THE LIGHT
CITY
IN THE

Why Christians Must Advance and Not Retreat

JANET & CRAIG PARSHALL

A
JANET
THOMA
BOOK

THOMAS NELSON PUBLISHERS
Nashville

Published in Nashville, Tennessee, by Thomas Nelson, Inc.

Unless otherwise noted, Scripture quotations are from the NEW AMERICAN STANDARD BIBLE®, © Copyright The Lockman Foundation 1960, 1962, 1963, 1968, 1971, 1972, 1973, 1975, 1977, 1995. Used by permission. (www.Lockman.org)

Scripture quotations noted NKJV are from THE NEW KING JAMES VERSION. Copyright © 1979, 1980, 1982, Thomas Nelson, Inc., Publishers.

Library of Congress Cataloging-in-Publication Data

Parshall, Craig, 1950–
        The light in the city : why Christians should advance and not retreat / Craig and Janet Parshall.
                p. cm.
        Includes bibliographical references.
        ISBN 0-7852-6890-1 (pbk.)
                1. United States—Religion—1960– 2. Christianity and culture—United States.
        3. Christian life—United States. I. Parshall, Janet, 1950– II. Title
BR526 .P36 2000
261'.1'0973—dc21

Printed in the United States of America
1 2 3 4 5 6 QWD 05 04 03 02 01 00

We dedicate this book to the past, present, and future travelers on the pilgrimage of the Christian faith who yearn for the City of God but nevertheless take up the challenging task of living out the gospel in the cities of man.

In particular, we wish to remember the powerful examples set by people such as John Witherspoon in colonial America and William Wilberforce in nineteenth-century England who so effectively applied the truth of the unchanging gospel to the moral and social hurricanes of their day.

We also dedicate this book to those fellow pilgrims who, in the waning years of the twentieth century and at the dawn of the twenty-first century, have been such powerful role models for the two of us in standing for truth and engaging the current culture for the cause of Christ.

But we also want to celebrate and acknowledge the next generation to come: those who refuse to retreat when the climate of opinion blows cold, who believe biblical truth to the marrow of their bones, and who will not be moved from their steadfast allegiance to the King of kings. May their tribe increase!

Contents

Acknowledgments

We must first say thanks to the good people at Thomas Nelson Publishers—in particular Janet Thoma, Michael Hyatt, and Rolf Zettersten—for their support of this book. We thank them particularly for their belief that its central premise deserves an exploration that is not only imaginative and interesting but intellectually rigorous as well. It is our hope and prayer that *The Light in the City* has accomplished that.

We want to extend a heartfelt thanks for those who passed on information and research that helped us with this book, which ran the full gamut from the scholarly to the more mundane, including locating that one piece of paper, that certain audiotape, those final legal citations, or that essential but misplaced book. In that regard we appreciate the efforts of Moriah Thompson, Caryn Collier, John Berhahya, and Marilyn Clifton.

Typing and proofreading help with portions of the manuscript came from Sharon and Darcey Donehey, to whom we are greatly appreciative. Also, thanks are due to Connie Reece and Anne Trudel for their skilled editing.

Our four children (as always) deserve acknowledgment for having "test-driven" many of the ideas in this book with us at our kitchen table. We also thank them for their support, encouragement, and partnership in the multitude of cultural/spiritual skirmishes to which the two of us have been called over the years. Most importantly, we appreciate their prayers and those of our parents, extended family, and all of those brothers and sisters in Christ who have graciously and consistently lifted us up before the throne of grace.

Once to every man and nation
Comes the moment to decide,
In the strife of truth with falsehood,
For the good or evil side;
Some great cause, some great decision*
Offering each the bloom or blight,
And the choice goes by forever,
'Twixt that darkness and that light.

—James Russell Lowell, 1844

---

*The original poem, "The Present Crisis," reads "God's new Messiah" in place of "some great decision."

Introduction

GREAT TRUTHS SOMETIMES disguise themselves in modest packages. In this nation one obscure little monument has a message for us—a message of tremendous importance. Few people have ever seen it. Yet, to the two of us, this unique place, like no other, brings home the fact that God granted America its charter of independence as a result of two separate, yet necessary, forces: the pragmatic efforts of men and women of *action*, as well as the spiritual vision of men and women of *faith*. Both of those forces—faith and action—were critical.

As the Church enters the twenty-first century, it faces a potent and critical question: How should Christians live out their faith in the midst of a culture that shows ever-increasing signs of decay and disintegration? In answering that question, we need to walk over to that historic yet obscure monument and learn from it.

We are not referring to the Lincoln Memorial, even though it is one of our personal favorites. The sense of power residing in that immense monument is hard to describe. You have to stand before the huge marble statue in person to feel its profound impact. The fact that we work in and around the Washington

Beltway has not diminished the monument's powerful grip. The two of us still journey there from time to time to walk up the great steps that bring us face to face with the giant presence of Abraham Lincoln. The force of that place comes from more than its sheer size or even the eloquent words of Lincoln chiseled into the high walls around him. Perhaps it is in the eyes. The sculptor captured the look of a man who knew the reality of suffering and the intense moral and political pressure that comes with the exercise of leadership in times of national crisis.

Neither are we referring to the Jefferson Memorial, although with its classical columns forming a perfect open-air rotunda, it is truly a magnificent expression of the architectural and intellectual brilliance of the Virginia statesman, drafter of the Declaration of Independence, and American president. As you look closer, you notice that Thomas Jefferson is standing in a field—a quiet reminder that this framer of American independence also took great pride in being a farmer.

There are hundreds of lesser-known monuments around the nation's capital city. Some are dedicated to the memories of our brave and fallen soldiers. Some memorialize the contributions of scientists, scholars, and artists; still others, diplomats and politicians. Collectively, they call us to appreciate the efforts of the many in forging a nation whose motto is still quite singular: One Nation Under God. No city on earth has more monuments dedicated to the ideal of political freedom than Washington, D.C. Yet, the monument we are referring to is not even located there.

We have in mind another monument, one not made with human hands. This modest and unassuming place is well hidden off a quiet residential street lined with trees and historical mansions in Fredericksburg, Virginia. A path takes you around a small replica of the Washington Monument—the place where Mary Washington, the mother of our first president, is buried. Then you duck beneath a canopy of hanging boughs and branches until you see a small hill. Jutting out from the top of the hill is a huge rock formation, split into two great planes of stone. This rocky table thrusts outward, overlooking the grassy descent below. The centuries have spotted this great stone ledge with green moss and lichen. This natural formation forms a smooth place to recline—or to pray.

This is Meditation Rock. It is the place where, during the dark days of the Revolutionary War, Mary Washington regularly came to pray for the safety of her son, General George Washington, and for the future of a country newly birthed yet fighting for its life. It is a quiet reminder of what too many have forgotten: Meditation Rock tells us that the birth of nations—and the freedoms bestowed upon their people—come from a God who intervenes in human affairs. But it also reminds us that our prayers to a sovereign God must be coupled with courageous action. In twenty-first-century America we are at risk of forgetting that the *faith* of the faithful and the *action* of men and women of goodwill must combine to roll back tyranny, to secure liberty, and to establish the welfare of our families, our churches, and our communities.

It would be easy to forget that. Economic prosperity threatens to turn the Church into a mere servant of the status quo—or even worse, into a silent, sofa-sitting witness to our national and individual moral decay. Further, a deadly air of defeatism threatens the evangelical community. Perhaps it was the inability of the United States Congress to remove a president who had so contemptuously violated his oath of office that delivered such a deadly message of discouragement. Was that failure the final pronouncement that conservative Christians were powerless to effect substantive cultural and moral change after all?

One of our reasons for writing this book is to dispel the specter of defeat looming over the conservative Christian movement. It's an area of concern that, in a sense, occupies the two of us full-time. Janet is host of *Janet Parshall's America*, a nationally syndicated talk show broadcast from Washington, D.C., and also the chief spokesperson for the Family Research Council. Craig is a trial lawyer in Virginia who argues cases around the nation involving religious and civil liberties and pro-family issues.

Another urgent reason for writing is to provide a counterpoint to the voices that have arisen from within the evangelical movement—voices that seem to call us to retreat. Well-intentioned though they may be, the questions raised by these voices must be answered. Their view of Christian citizenship and the need for the Church to de-emphasize the public affairs of this nation—and their call for Christians to question their support of groups and causes that engage the great questions of the day—must be taken seriously.

In fact, this question may be one of the most critical, and controversial, issues facing evangelical Christians at the beginning of our new century.

The first volley in this exchange of friendly fire within the ranks of Christian conservatives came shortly after the vote by the United States Senate, which failed to muster the necessary votes to convict William Jefferson Clinton of "high crimes and misdemeanors" and thereby remove him from office. Noted conservative Paul Weyrich released a statement that shocked Washington political insiders, journalists, and political activists of all stripes.

Paul Weyrich has been one of the key architects of the conservative wing of American politics for more than thirty years. He is the founder of the Free Congress Foundation, one of the intellectual framers of the Reagan Revolution, and a man whose conscience is guided by the best of Judeo-Christian ideals. A tough strategist and political realist, Weyrich has also been a role model for both of us.

In a statement released on the Free Congress Web site, Weyrich stated that politics in America has "failed because of the collapse of the culture," and that "we are caught up in a cultural collapse of historic proportions, a collapse so great that it simply overwhelms politics." In the end, "politics itself has failed" to turn America around, according to Weyrich.[1]

His remedy for conservative Christians is to create a cultural and social quarantine. He has suggested, in effect, that we build a kind of parallel political, social, and cultural universe, which will be "separate and free" from the decay of contemporary American politics. We should, "in every respect but politics . . . build a new nation among the ruins of the old."[2]

Though he has denied it, some have interpreted his comments as a call for hasty retreat. In truth, Weyrich has clarified his message several times, and it is clear that he is really calling for innovation but not resignation. It is clear to those of us who know him that Paul Weyrich has shown no signs of giving up on the battle for the mind, heart, and soul of America. Yet the image portrayed in the press was that the conservative (and particularly the Christian conservative) movement was unraveling.

No sooner had this issue hit the mainstream media ("Social Conservatives' Ties to GOP Fraying," cried the front-page headline in the *Washington Post*[3]) than a second maelstrom struck the Washington Beltway. This second one had reverberations that spread out with concentric shock waves to Christian churches everywhere. Of course, the secular media were only too pleased to report it.

Cal Thomas, a noted conservative columnist, an evangelical Christian, and a good personal friend, released his newest book, *Blinded by Might.* He coauthored the book with Michigan pastor and former member of the Moral Majority Ed Dobson (no relation to Dr. James Dobson).

Blinded by Might is, to a large degree, an indictment of the tactics and the failures of the religious right wing in America. It is filled with anecdotes of Cal Thomas from his years as a key player in the Moral Majority. It is also a call for Christians to reflect on the relationship between the Christian church, with its primary call to evangelize, and the rough-and-tumble world of modern hardball politics.

Thomas notes:

> Modern politics has become so corrupting that virtually every political movie coming out of Hollywood in recent years has viewed politics through a thick lens of cynicism . . .
>
> Is this the kind of process in which conservative Christians ought to immerse themselves? And if so—if they must descend to this level of politics—can they really be said to be serving a greater kingdom and a greater King?[4]

Again, Cal Thomas and Ed Dobson are quick to remind us that they are not arguing for a "complete withdrawal from politics." Yet their book argues consistently that Christian conservatives have accomplished nothing in the last decades of the so-called "culture war." More importantly, they spend an entire book arguing that groups like the Moral Majority were powerless to effect any real change. At the same time, they have offered no reason why Christians should not retreat to potluck church suppers and programs that define the Great Commission and evangelism in only the most *narrow* and isolated terms. The implication is that Christians should not sully their hands with the public issues that threaten to destroy our nation.

Elsewhere in their book, Thomas and Dobson bluntly conclude that the Christian faith and the world of politics are mutually exclusive and can never really be reconciled. They base this conclusion on the premise that these two activities operate from different underlying principles, which are in conflict with one another. Faith requires total obedience to the will of God. Politics, on the other hand, swims in the unsanitary petri dish of compromise, where moral principle almost always comes in a poor second.

Here is how they put it:

> In politics, zealotry is often seen as fanaticism. Politics is about compromise, and goals are mostly achieved in increments. Politics and faith are irreconcilable. The former cannot tolerate zealotry; the latter cannot tolerate compromise. [5]

Other voices are joining this call for a rethinking of Christian involvement in public affairs. Erwin Lutzer, pastor of Moody Church, has written a book titled *Why the Cross Can Do What Politics Can't*. The title articulates the position inside his book: that the power of the gospel of Jesus Christ is antithetical to the corrupting and ultimately impotent powers of the political and cultural realm.

This is no mere abstract discussion among seminary professors or Washington insiders. A fierce debate is brewing, and it has become increasingly public. In addition to the Christian press (*Christianity Today* has run a cover story titled "Is the Religious Right Finished?"[6]), the secular media has made this one of the major issues of the current election cycle. The future of Christian conservatives has been the topic of *60 Minutes* and the *New York Times*.

Of course, there is nothing entirely new about questioning the alignment of the evangelical church with political or social issues. For years we have had the same question asked of us from Christians at almost every place where we engage public issues: Is it really appropriate to mix the gospel with all of these political activities?

The difference now is that leaders within the evangelical and conservative camp are seriously asking this question. Furthermore, this question is being asked at a critical time in American history. Today our country is at a perilous crossroads. We have been forced to endure almost thirty years of legalized abortion. Television, cinema, and Internet indecency have never been more outrageous. The president of our nation, through his conduct in office, has disgraced our national discourse about the office he occupies. Attacks on the legitimacy of traditional family life and the institution of marriage have never been bolder or more aggressive. Even the freedom and autonomy of our institutions of faith are being challenged by the long regulatory arm of the government.

Some evangelicals have hoped for a time of coming together— of finding common ground between the combatants in the culture war in America as we enter the new century. Such hopes seemed dim, however, when the White House chose to condemn the entire Southern Baptist Convention just a few days prior to the end of the twentieth century. White House Press Secretary Joe Lockhart articulated the position of President Clinton that the plan of Southern Baptists to share the gospel with Muslims and Hindus placed Baptists in the category of groups that "perpetuate ancient religious hatred."[7] Lockhart's comments reiterated the president's view that the great challenge of the twenty-first century was to stamp out "intolerance . . . and religious hatred." Apparently no thought was given that such statements, aimed at Bible-believing Christians by the most powerful political office on the planet, were themselves examples of "religious hatred." It is no overstatement to say that the Clinton administration's statements against the Southern Baptist view of the Great Commission represents one of the most outrageous White House attacks against evangelicals in our time.

How should conservative Christians respond to the hostility against them? How should we engage a culture that shows every sign of collapsing in on itself? In a larger sense, these are not even intrinsically "American" questions—nor are they even questions that concern only the American Christian church. With the fall of communism in Central and Eastern Europe, something powerful and fascinating started to happen. Within the democracies that began to emerge, the underground Christian population began to emerge as well. Like those who have survived in caves during the reign of tyranny and oppression above ground, Christians in these countries are now coming to the surface. They are yearning for answers on how to stand for the gospel; yet, at the same time, they want to know how to run their nations in freedom, truth, and prosperity. They are watching us. They are waiting to see how Christians in the most successful democracy of the past two thousand years will engage an ever-decaying political, moral, and social culture in the new millennium.

What example are we setting for Christians around the globe?

None of us knows what will happen in China. Few of us could have predicted Tienanmen Square. The pro-democracy movement is not dead there. We know that the Christian church movement is alive and well in China, but it is suffering greatly. If democratic reforms begin surfacing there in the decades to come, what example will we have provided to China's evangelicals? Pro-democracy demonstrations have actually begun breaking out in Iran—one of the darkest examples of Islamic autocracy in the world. If the door to the gospel is opened there, what prototype of Christian citizenship will we have created for them by our actions in the coming months and years?

This is neither a question of politics, nor is it a question of political elections or political parties. Rather, this is a question that goes to the very core of what it means to be a Christian.

In 1981 Francis Schaeffer wrote *A Christian Manifesto*. It was a groundbreaking and controversial work. Asked about the writing of that book, Schaeffer stated that he saw America nearing a crossroads. He predicted that an unrevived and unreformed America might follow in the footsteps of Nazi Germany. Schaeffer was still calling Christians to apply the logic, the power, and the truth of the gospel to the lives of unsaved individuals. But he was also calling Christians to apply the truth of the gospel to the workings of government and to the crumbling foundations of fallen culture. He sought to expand the influence of the saving message of Jesus Christ—not constrict it.

In the following pages we will try to determine whether that vision was right or wrong. We will strive to answer the question that was raised several decades ago but which has yet to be concisely and pragmatically answered: In the light of the revealed truth of Christ, and in the midst of our present generation, how shall we then live?

1 | Mining for Truth:
The Real Program Behind the Politics

BEFORE WE CAN evaluate how we respond as Christians to our ever-changing cultural environment in the beginning of the twenty-first century, we must come to grips with two realities.

First, we have to realize that everyone has a worldview—a particular set of presuppositions through which he or she views the world. A recent encounter, in particular, illustrated this for the two of us. We had been in Orlando, Florida, to attend a bookseller's convention to kick off our first book. It was interesting and exciting but also very exhausting. It had been a full day of running from one radio or video interview to another.

That day a story began running on the news wires saying that young teenagers (thirteen- and fourteen-year-olds) in one particular city were having regularly scheduled "oral sex parties." One of the teens interviewed reportedly responded that if it was all right for the president of the United States, why not for them? The teens felt that oral sex was perfectly appropriate—there was no chance of getting pregnant and little or no chance of contracting AIDS.

One thing we've learned about the media business is that there is no such thing as a day off. A national television program tracked Janet down at the convention center and asked if she could come on the program that night. She would be debating Joycelyn Elders, President Clinton's former surgeon general. They offered to uplink her part of the interview by satellite from a facility at Universal Studios, just a twenty-minute drive from our hotel. We enlisted some hasty prayer support from friends at the convention and then ran out to the limo the station had sent to pick us up.

A SURGEON GENERAL AND A LIMO DRIVER:
TWO WORLDVIEWS

The limo driver was a friendly, talkative fellow who got us there in plenty of time. Janet's part of the interview consisted of looking into a television camera in a small, bare room. Usually a monitor sits on the floor showing what the whole program from New York would look like—what the audience would see—but in this case, there wasn't even a monitor. There was just the single eye of a camera on a tripod and an earplug to supply Janet with the audio.

The former surgeon general gave the same responses to the issue of teenage sexuality that she had when she ignited a national furor while serving in the Clinton administration. As long as these kids minimized the risks of pregnancy and AIDS, she saw no problem with their exercising creativity in finding new and different ways to gratify themselves. After all, Elders speculated, these young people are going to have sex anyway—which is why, she concluded, they needed comprehensive sex education.

"My dog doesn't need instruction on how to have sex," Janet responded. "Lack of education is not the root problem."

Joyceyln Elders's worldview was as open, obvious, and as

incredibly misguided as it had ever been, when it came to the idea of how to deal with teen sexuality.

When the program was over, the limo driver showed up and we jumped in the back. We drove through the muggy, hot Florida evening for a few moments, and then the driver struck up a conversation. Small talk soon turned to bigger issues. Before long, he was telling us about his background. He had received little formal education beyond junior high school. But he was a voracious reader, and it was clear that he had done a good job of educating himself on a wide variety of subjects.

He said that at one time he had concluded that most, if not all, of the world's problems were a result of problems in the environment in which people were nurtured. Change the environment, he reasoned, and you can change people.

As we exited the freeway and started heading into the hotel district of Orlando, our driver continued to explain his ideas, his voice becoming increasingly excited. He went on to say that he had continued to read further on the subject, and that he had since changed his mind. Now he believed that almost all human behavior is linked to genetics and DNA. All we have to do, he indicated, is to use genetic engineering to breed out the problem areas of human conduct.

"Except for one thing," Craig said. "If you believe that there is such a thing as sin inherent in the human condition, then genetic engineering won't solve the problem. If that is where evil comes from, then we have to look for a solution to sin somewhere other than science or genetic engineering."

Our driver grew quiet and then changed the subject as we drove through the darkness. Finally we pulled into the luminous driveway of the front portico of the hotel. We both got out and gave him a warm good-bye.

A little later it struck us how well-developed the worldviews of both a former surgeon general and a limo driver had been that night. In fact, both worldviews came from a similar position.

Joycelyn Elders looked at teenagers as merely biological entities, whose conduct was predictable and unpreventable. Sex was just one more biological fact to manipulate and control. Because her view of teens ultimately leads to seeing them as mere beasts of the field—as always prone, by nature, to sexual promiscuity—the real question is how we can best clean up after them, *not* how we might lead them to wholesome and moral lives. In that worldview, moral rules are irrelevant.

In the same way, our limo driver looked at people as biological entities whose behavior was predictable and preprogrammed. Regardless of whether it was environment or genetics that did the programming, the driver's worldview was clear: in the words of Francis Schaeffer, this fellow had come to the conclusion that humans, at the most basic level, are the result of a "combination of time plus matter plus chance." When we started challenging the limo driver's assumption by suggesting that there may be a spiritual reality behind the reality of evil in the world, his worldview was threatened, and he closed the discussion.

There is also a second reality that we need to consider: Our worldviews have a real and powerful effect on our actions. In other words, to borrow from the title of Richard Weaver's influential book: *Ideas Have Consequences.*

Weaver pointed out eloquently the problem with the "apostles of modernism" (here we could insert most academic institutions; most contemporary "intellectuals"—artists, musicians, writers, and philosophers; and most political scientists and politicians). The problem, he noted, is that they have rushed toward a worldview based on empiricism, the belief that the only reliable guide to evaluating the world is our sensory data alone. As such, the "seers" of our current generation have almost entirely ignored "first principles."[1] Weaver argued that if we are really interested in the pursuit of truth, then we must decide our first principles at the outset.

First principles are the basic logical, moral, and theological rules about human nature, society, right and wrong, and our accountability before God. Without these first principles, we are unable to apply reasonable rules to our conduct or the conduct of others. When that happens, we are unable to govern others—or ourselves—according to a common core of values. Social disintegration is the awful by-product.

Empiricism has been one of the prevailing philosophies of the twentieth century. With the rise of the scientific method and its emphasis on "observed" sensory data, radical empiricism—the view that reason and scientific observation can solve all problems—has crowded out other philosophies to the point where it has achieved a virtual monopoly, even an unthinking one, in the field of ideas. Radical empiricism has even won an intellectual foothold among Christians, and it seems to be a prevailing concept in America.

Looking at the developing life of an embryonic human in the first trimester from a purely empirical standpoint tells us very little about the ultimate humanity of that preborn infant. Most scientists and doctors will tell you that a ten-week-old preborn baby has all of the basic functions of a fully human person: it has all of the basic DNA of a complete human, and there is also reliable data that the nervous system of such a preborn baby is capable of feeling pain. So, why aren't the radical empiricists of our age crying out against the inhumanity of abortion? The reason, among others, is that defining *humanity* requires the application of more than mere scientific observation. It involves, ultimately, the application of first principles, including the principle that, as the Declaration of Independence states, our Creator is the one who bestows upon us the right to life.

In the context of abortion, the fallacy of empiricism became coupled with the drive for self-fulfillment at any cost. It was also aided by a national lust for individual autonomy, and finally with the disregard for the traditional moral teachings of the Bible. The result was a twentieth-century America that gave birth to a doctrine of death, practiced, ironically, by healers whose Hippocratic oath requires them to protect life. This doctrine of death was justified by lawgivers who have neglected the basic laws of the Lawgiver. Lastly, it was rationalized by many mainline religious leaders who turned the principles of the Bible upside down.

The radical doctrine of empiricism, a favorite among humanists, is at odds with the Judeo-Christian view of the world. This was pointed out by Edward O. Wilson, a social evolutionist, who was awarded the 1999 Humanist of the Year Award by the American Humanist Association. In his acceptance speech Wilson noted that the conflict between empiricism (the idea that all we can know is found in the natural world) and transcendentalism (the belief in spiritual realities that "transcend" our natural senses) "will be the twenty-first century's version of the struggle for the human soul." Wilson concluded, "I believe also that the winner of this struggle will be empiricism."[2]

Where will the Church be in this great struggle of the twenty-first century? Where will our elected representatives stand on the matter of first principles? How will Christians respond to the radical empiricism of American culture? The moral, spiritual, and social presuppositions of our public officials and cultural leaders do count. Character has always counted.

HILLARY AND BILL: A CASE STUDY

Barbara Olson, a former federal prosecutor and popular media commentator, was researching her new book on the life and times of Hillary Clinton when she appeared as a guest on *Janet Parshall's America*. Olson revealed that Hillary Clinton entered college as a moderately conservative Republican. She came out as a radical. What was the catalyst for this dramatic left turn?

According to Olson, Hillary Clinton became greatly influenced during those years by the thinking of the '60s political guru Saul Alinsky. Alinsky was a labor organizer and radical activist. He also became one of the primary intellectual forces behind the strategies of political radicalism in the 1960s and 1970s.

Hillary Clinton was introduced to Alinsky in Chicago after graduation from college. The two soon forged an ideological relationship, and Alinsky offered Hillary a job as an intern. The only reason she turned him down was apparently the fact that she had decided to go to law school. It is now clear, based on Barbara Olson's research, that Hillary made this socialist radical the centerpiece of her thesis at Wellesley College. When her husband was sworn in as president, her alma mater quickly put her research thesis under lock and key. Yet Hillary openly admitted her affinity to Alinsky in a 1993 *Washington Post* interview.[3]

As a result of Barbara Olson's revelation into the Alinsky–Hillary connection, we decided to brush up on our research into Saul Alinsky. Both of us were college students in the late 1960s and were familiar with his fame among the radical intelligentsia on America's campuses. Alinsky was considered a revolutionary prophet for groups like Students for a Democratic Society (SDS). In his book *Rules for Radicals*, Alinsky defined the essence of true radicalism and revealed how radicalism should hold orthodox Christianity in contempt. He gave a glowing acknowledgment in his book to "Lucifer, the very first radical" . . . "the first radical known to man who rebelled against the establishment and did it so effectively that he at least won his own kingdom."[4]

In Alinsky's view, there are two forces that are the enemies of the radical left. One is Madison Avenue, with its "middle-class moral hygiene." The other is "organized religion, which has espoused a rhetoric of 'turning the other cheek' and has quoted the Scriptures," all in supposed pursuit of its perceived function in "supporting the establishment."[5]

This kind of radical devotion to social restructuring (and rejection of the Judeo-Christian worldview) can be found in Hillary Clinton's own political philosophy. In her earlier writings in law review articles, she suggested a revolutionary new view toward children's rights. This idea was continued (in a milder and more moderate form, of course) in her book, *It Takes a Village*. The title reflects the African proverb, quoted often by liberals and social engineers, that it "takes a whole village to raise a child." The real message of Mrs. Clinton's book is that all of our children belong to everyone. This message may sound good in a socialist system, but it is inconsistent with the idea that appears throughout Scripture—that God blesses parents, not the state, with children. It is interesting to note that Jesus indicated that one of the signs of the end times will be that "children will rise up"—not against the state, but "against parents" (Matt. 10:21 NKJV). According to the Bible, one of the ultimate signs of social disintegration and final doom is an antagonistic and hostile separation of children from their parents and family.

Likewise, Hillary Clinton's worldview on abortion and women's rights were a clear indicator that she was a proponent of radical feminism. In 1990, two years before her husband would be elected president of the United States, Hillary Clinton was helping to promote a proabortion takeover of the American Bar Association (ABA).

In the months prior to the August 1990 annual convention of the ABA, a coalition of legal groups supporting full and unfettered abortion rights had been gathering support for a controversial resolution. The actual recommendation was so radical that it not only called for official ABA endorsement of abortion, but it also demanded taxpayer funding of abortions for indigent women who might have problems financing the procedure. The proabortion report of this coalition was submitted in the name, among others, of Hillary Rodham Clinton, in her position as chair of the Commission on Women in the Profession. In the wake of the proabortion lobbying by Clinton *et al.*, the ABA went on record in 1990 with its first full and official endorsement of the awful decision in *Roe v. Wade*.

In retrospect, America had every reason to have been just as skeptical about Bill Clinton as about Hillary. If our churches had taken seriously his worldview in 1992, we could have foreseen the insults he was about to inflict on the American presidency.

It is beyond dispute that if the majority of evangelicals had voted in the 1992 presidential election, and if a solid majority of those had voted for Bob Dole rather than Bill Clinton, Mr. Clinton would not have been elected. This is not to say that Bob Dole was a good choice for evangelical Christians. His campaign ignored evangelicals, and he avoided taking clear stands on the moral issues of the day. But while he might have done little good, at least he would have done little harm. In retrospect, it seems clear that, despite the fact that he was able to ride a national economic upswing, Bill Clinton was a terrible choice for Bible-believing Christians and for America as well.

It all started with the traditional pomp and ceremony. On a crisp January day in Washington in 1993, William Jefferson Clinton put one hand on the Bible and raised the other high in the air. Before the Chief Justice of the Supreme Court, and before a watching world, Mr. Clinton took the oath of office. With flags snapping smartly in the wind, and surrounded by the echoes of marching bands and the full trappings of Americana, Mr. Clinton promised us a "coming together"—an American reunion.

Then, two short days later, on the twentieth anniversary of the decision of the Supreme Court in *Roe v. Wade*, President Bill Clinton—with the stroke of his pen, and seemingly empowered by the votes of the American people—swept into oblivion *five* separate executive orders that had previously restricted and limited abortion. During the election Mr. Clinton and his stalwart proabortion supporters had been trumpeting a familiar tune. All they wanted, we were told, was to make abortion "safe and rare."

President Clinton's new executive orders, signed into law while the boxes were still being unpacked in the White House, opened the door for the abortifacient drug RU-486 to be privately imported onto American shores. He also removed Title X regulations that had been in place to prevent any federal funding to clinics that counseled abortion as an option. Mr. Clinton also paved the way that day for abortions to be performed at military hospitals, and for testing to be done on fetal tissue.

Lastly, in a move that would be a prognostication of Mr. Clinton's new pro-China policy, he reversed our nation's prior refusal to use taxpayer money to support China's brutal forced abortion, one-child-per-family policy through our funding of the United Nations Population Fund (UNFPA).

During Bill Clinton's first term, Craig filed a lawsuit against the Clinton administration on behalf of Congressman Chris

Smith and two Chinese nationals who had escaped aboard the notorious ship *Golden Venture*. In the lawsuit, filed in the U.S. District Court of the District of Columbia through The Rutherford Institute, Craig challenged the interpretation the Clinton administration had placed on Congressional restrictions on the funding of UNFPA. The Clinton administration had lowered almost all barriers to sending U.S. tax dollars to a UN effort that would give aid and comfort to China's barbaric abortion policies. State Department information and other well-documented sources clearly showed that in some cases Chinese women had been handcuffed and dragged into abortion clinics by physical force.

Internal memos of the administration showed that massive American funding of the UN agency that assisted China in its population control efforts was, in the opinion of Clinton bureaucrats, all but a foregone conclusion. This was in direct conflict with a law passed by Congress, the Kemp-Kasten Amendment, which clearly prohibited such funding if it assisted China's policy of forced abortions and forced sterilization.

At the very same time that President Clinton was feting Chinese President Jiang Zemin in his effort to court Asian-Pacific trade, French news agencies were reporting that China's abortion atrocities had actually escalated. In the Hunan province, death sentences were being passed down for persons who merely *assisted* a woman in avoiding forced abortion. Craig filed evidence of these reports with the federal court and with the Justice Department, which was defending the Clinton administration in the suit. Yet Mr. Clinton, who must have been aware of these atrocities—they were known to his own State Department—avoided any mention of this human rights outrage in his meetings with China's top communist leader.

Ultimately the lawsuit, which had put a hold on some twenty million U.S. dollars to the UNFPA, forced a tightening up of the policies within the Clinton administration. It restricted, for a while, the conditions under which the U.S. could fund the UN population programs. In the end, however, President Clinton continued to willfully ignore human rights violations in China. Such violations involved not only forced abortion but the continuous persecution of Christians as well.

Since that time Mr. Clinton has continued to lavish trade perks on China, including the exportation of computer technology. He has lobbied successfully for that country to receive Most Favored Nation (MFN) trade status and permanent trade status despite its abysmal human rights record. Beyond even that, questions still remain about the relationship between President Clinton, the Democratic Party, and illegal campaign funds traced to China.

When Bill Clinton aggressively sought election funding from gay and lesbian groups during his first bid for the presidency, we should have been forewarned. After the election there was a virtual prohomosexual takeover of Washington, D.C. during Gay Pride Week. Closed-circuit television sets in federal offices played an endless listing of prohomosexual events. During the Clinton administration, criticism of the gay lifestyle in government and military offices in Washington has become one of the few forms of censored speech. To air those opinions is viewed as an open invitation for the speaker to lose his or her place on the career ladder, or suffer formal discipline, or worse. Both of us have received clandestine reports from Washington agency officials and military officers about the prohomosexual overhaul that was taking place. We had to meet secretly with many of them because they had no doubt that they would be sanctioned or fired if it were made known that they were whistle-blowers.

Mr. Clinton's allegiance to his homosexual funding base was later illustrated by his notorious "Don't Ask, Don't Tell" policy, which permitted homosexuals to serve in the military as long as they did not voluntarily disclose their sexual orientation.

More recently the Clinton administration approved a listing in the National Register of Historic Places for the former Stonewall Inn in Greenwich Village. The Inn was the site of a violent uprising of homosexuals and lesbians, who hurled bottles and other assorted missiles and screamed obscenities at the police. Thus was the "noble" beginning of the modern gay rights movement; and now, thanks to Bill Clinton, it is memorialized in American history with the imprimatur and support of our federal government.

Al Gore is following in the footsteps of his boss. In the early stages of electioneering, Mr. Gore paid a supportive visit to the Los Angeles Gay and Lesbian Center, America's largest homosexual community center, as part of his fund-raising swing through California. The visit came two days after Mr. Gore had delivered a speech stressing his "own values of faith and family."[6]

Is it appropriate that evangelicals question Al Gore's real agenda? Of course it is. We must question the real agenda of Al Gore as much as we need to analyze the ultimate worldviews of every other candidate. If we fail to do so, we have invested in fool's gold: we have bought the notion that election promises and campaign ads tell us what is really important, and that bedrock beliefs and below-radar values of a candidate make no difference. But to quote the wisdom of Proverbs: "For as he thinks within himself, so he is" (Prov. 23:7).

WILL THE REAL CULTURE WAR PLEASE STAND UP?

When we move from the worldviews of particular national leaders to the broad spectrum of America's landscape of beliefs, we enter a kind of demilitarized zone. Here, like the thirty-eighth parallel separating North and South Korea, there is a kind of standoff in America over cherished ideals. For the last decade or so there has been a lot written about something called a "culture war" in America. By that, we mean a clash of beliefs about moral, spiritual, and social issues—a clash so basic and fundamental that the two sides predict catastrophically divergent scenarios for our nation depending on whose vision will prevail. In this culture war we are no longer debating whether the umpire mistakenly called as a "strike" what was really a "ball" in the World Series of ideas. Instead, we are questioning whether there can be a correct definition of a "strike" at all. Who wins is no longer the point; in a culture war we are debating whether the well-worn rules of the game should be thrown out altogether.

Some of our conservative comrades in arms now question whether there really ever was a true culture war in America in the first place. Professor Jeremy Rabkin, writing in the conservative *Policy Review*, published by the Heritage Foundation, concludes that all this talk of culture wars has been a gross distortion. Rabkin thinks that it is "dangerous" and "self-defeating" for religious conservatives in particular to place emphasis on the vision of an "overriding culture war" in our nation.[7]

Other commentators recognize the reality of a culture war but are busy trying to fashion a truce. Sociologist James Davison Hunter sees hope in the possibility of a more civil discourse and in creating common ground among battling forces.[8] Tom Sine, who has taught at Fuller Theological Seminary, urges us to find not only a cease-fire in the battle of ideas and beliefs, but urges us to see beyond the "us" and "them" mentality and to adopt "a third way." He praises a semimonastic Christian community in Australia and a similar community approach in Woodcrest, New York as two examples of peacemaking.[9]

Is there is a real and present culture war that calls for our personal and committed engagement? If we don't like the answer to that question, then we must either deny that the conflict exists, or look for ways around it—anything except enter the fray; any way but the way of confrontation.

To us, there is only one solution (albeit one that has many different strategies): We must lovingly, but firmly, commend what is good, and we must also confront what is evil, armed with God's unyielding truth and motivated by His supernatural love.

Every so often we are reminded of the importance of this personal resolve. Every so often we see, once again, the alarming decline of freedom, and witness the storm clouds gathering in the distance.

One small but startling example came recently from one of the listeners to Janet's radio program. That listener, like many of us, enjoys the vast opportunities of interactive communication on the Internet.

He explained how he was involved in an Internet chat room called Christian Forum. It is important to note that this was labeled as a *Christian* chat room.

The discussion in this particular Internet forum turned to homosexuality. Janet's listener, a Christian, typed into the electronic dialogue some comments about the subject to the effect that "it is a choice to participate in a nonheterosexual manner," and that homosexual conduct is a matter of personal choice, "just like pedophilia is a choice," or "just like abortion is a choice," or just like "alcoholism is a choice."

Shortly after this computer dialogue, Janet's listener received an e-mail reprimand from his Internet service provider (ISP).

The listener was reminded of the Terms of Service agreement the ISP uses to control the content of computer dialogue, and he was informed that the Internet provider had received a complaint about his comments on homosexuality.

Now, it should be remembered that the Supreme Court *struck down* a federal law that attempted to control the accessibility of pornography to minors over the Internet. The High Court ruled in 1997 that provisions of the Communications Decency Act of 1996 that prohibited persons from sending sexually "indecent" material over the Internet, where such materials would be available to children, violated the First Amendment.[10] Yet, at the same time, a Christian user of the Internet is attacked for voicing his opinions on the issue of homosexuality in a "Christian" chat room. In the pornography example, free expression is protected as an ultimate good, even at the cost of exposing children to outrageous and harmful indecency. In the chat room example, the promotion of tolerance of homosexuality is the virtue; the free expression of the Christian is of lesser consequence.

There is a way, of course, to explain this strange anomaly of different outcomes from a strictly legal standpoint. The First Amendment applies only when there is official governmental action of some kind. In the pornography example, Congress had passed a law—and that law was an act of government sufficient to permit the Supreme Court to apply the protections of the First Amendment.

On the other hand, it could be argued that the tiff between the Christian Internet user and his Internet service provider was a private affair—a private contractual relationship. Thus, with no formal governmental action involved, the First Amendment was of no avail.

Yet while that may provide a *legal* answer, it does not solve the bigger *moral* dilemma: We are living in a society that is increasingly tolerant of the most incredible depictions of violence and sexual barbarism. At the same time we are, as a culture, becoming more and more intolerant of those, particularly Christians, who voice objections to morally questionable conduct, such as homosexuality or abortion.

House Majority Leader Dick Armey recently gave an address in the House of Representatives that listed countless examples of recent anti-Christian bigotry on a national scale. Among the examples cited were (1) the reluctance of Janet Reno's Justice Department to label things like the church shootings of Christians in Fort Worth, Texas, as "hate crimes," while at the same time jumping to the aid of those who call the killings of minorities or homosexuals hate crimes; (2) a federal juvenile counseling program that warns officials that children may be particularly dangerous if they are raised in a "very religious" home; and (3) the *Denver Post*'s rabid criticisms of the Christian aspects of the memorial service for the slain teens of Littleton, Colorado, despite the fact that a high proportion of those targeted for murder were outspoken evangelical Christians.[11]

Those who, like Professor Rabkin, doubt the validity of a real culture war in America might respond that our Internet example presents an unusual and extreme case. Those of us who have been in the trenches of this conflict know better. These "anomalies" are becoming so frequent that it is hard to ignore the pattern they present: the nurse that Craig and a Philadelphia-area lawyer represented, who was fired by a supervisor (a self-proclaimed supporter of the homosexual group ACT UP) because she was a born-again Christian; countless ACLU lawsuits that have stripped countless traditional symbols of faith from our public landscape; the ongoing battle by the National Education

Association (NEA) establishment and church–state separationists to halt the expansion of "school choice" programs that would include religious schools; the erosion of parental rights and the arrogance of public school officials who transport children to abortion clinics without notifying their families; the current suggestion by modern moral philosophers who seek to justify forms of infanticide. One of the evidences that the moral conflict in America is real is the fact that institutional America is becoming steadfastly intolerant of those persons who freely articulate the tenets of traditional biblical Christianity or who passionately defend pre-born life. This new intolerance represents a massive shift of values over the last half century.

Thus, the real question is not *whether* there is a culture war, or *whether* Christians should enlist. Those questions have long been settled for any of us who have spent a substantial time occupying the embattled foxholes. The real question is *how* and *where* we should do battle so as to fulfill the commands of God's Word and to advance His kingdom. A good beginning point is recognizing that while this is a battle, it is not a battle merely of flesh and blood. Rather, this is a spiritual battle to be fought in God's power and consistent with His purposes.

Yet to recognize where the battle must be waged, we must appreciate the importance of the worldviews maintained by the spokespersons of our culture. As we have seen in this chapter, some of those spokespersons profess to speak for America. As we will see in the next chapter, some of them profess to speak for God.

2 | Why Things Are Not Right with the Religious Left

IMAGINE THAT ONE night you plop down on the sofa in your family room. You click on the television and begin surfing the channels. You come to the PBS station, where a man on a small stage catches your attention. The lecturer, you are told, is Dr. Wayne Dyer, and he is addressing a small audience in the studio. The set is sparse but friendly. Dr. Dyer is dressed informally—no tie, with an open-collared shirt and a sweater. He looks friendly, and his tone is warm, accepting, and informal. His style of speech is conversational, nontechnical, and, above all, sincere.

Dr. Dyer assures his audience that he is not part of any formal movement or organization. His message is simply a personal one, gained from his own experience. This is, he explains, a message that he hopes will help his audience gain the kind of life they really want. Again, he reassures his audience that he is not part of any organized movement. The message is becoming clear. The audience can be reassured that this is no televangelist or Christian huckster. No, indeed. Dr. Dyer, a psychologist by profession, gives us the powerful impression that he will not be pushing any dogma at all.

However, as you watch and listen from the comfort of your own home, Dr. Dyer will be sharing some of the most effective psuedoreligious dogma that the religious left has to offer. Unlike the religious right, the religious left has escaped any organizational labels. Its appearance has been largely undetected in the press, and its spiritual doctrines sound highly individualistic and libertarian, thus creating the illusion that what we have here is merely some friendly spiritual banter, but not a full-blown "movement." We know of no prominent attacks, in the secular press, of PBS's use of Dr. Dyer to evangelize the American public with a new gospel of inner peace.

THE REALITY OF THE RELIGIOUS LEFT

Though the PBS program featuring Wayne Dyer presents itself as self-help transformational psychology, it is actually providing a thoroughly spiritual perspective on life. Aided by our federal tax dollars, PBS is using the lectures of pop-gurus like Dr. Dyer to proselytize America with a new-left theology that is one of the major challengers to historic Christian truth.

Dr. Dyer slowly walks back and forth before his smiling audience. He explains the path to a "higher" awareness in life. He shares his message of personal transformation, which increasingly begins to sound more like theology than self-help psychology.

Two factors make Dr. Dyer a prime example of the new religious left. First is the theological content of his message. As an alternative to the historic Christian faith, his approach hammers away at the dangers of moral judgmentalism, which he suggests is the thing that creates "toxic thinking." The true path embraced by Dyer is an amalgamation of pop psychology, Buddhism, and religious mysticism. His writings quote from sources such as Buddha, Zen, Rumi (a Sufi mystic), Meister Eckhart, and *A Course in Miracles.* The reality of sin (and the need of a Savior) is absent in his psychospirituality. God is in everyone—and everyone is essentially divine. According to Dr. Dyer, all we have to do is tap into the divine nature that inhabits us all:

> There is not a separate God for each person. There is one universal intelligence flowing through all of us.
>
> That is the force of love. Remind yourself of that every time you doubt your own divinity. Affirm to yourself that you are divine and that you love and are loved and will not be pressured by your false-thinking ego to not know this. Remind yourself that the same force flows through you that flowed through Jesus Christ and Buddha.[1]

The second thing that puts Dr. Dyer in the camp of the religious left is the way in which PBS, the unofficial public information service for American liberalism, has embraced his message. Not only is his message televised, but he also makes personal appearances on PBS fund-raising broadcasts, urging the viewers to contribute to the Public Broadcasting Service that he, himself, finds so enriching. Dyer's books and tapes are used as premiums and giveaways to those who send in their pledges.

In case there were any doubts about PBS's political agenda, all bets were settled when it was learned that more than thirty PBS affiliates had given their donor lists to the Democratic Party to generate political contributions. This kind of mind-melding between PBS and political liberalism had long been taken for granted. Many of us made this educated assumption based on the kind of standard fare one finds on PBS programming, particularly in the regular bashing of the religious right, and the overt promotion of the homosexual rights movement in shows like *In the*

Life. With the release of the donor lists, the political orientation of PBS is a proven fact.

PBS, supported by the political left, has in turn presented a spiritual perspective essentially at odds with biblical Christianity. Dr. Wayne Dyer is not the only religious prophet of the left who is showcased. PBS has also aired the lectures of eastern pop-mystic Deepak Chopra, who advances a brand of Hinduism that touts a mystical "Christ consciousness." It is an enticing concept, but when you study the philosophy of the man, you realize that he has no need for Christ as Savior because he does not see the existence of a sin problem in the world.

We cannot make the real case for Christians to advance, rather than retreat, from this culture war without addressing the significant influence of the religious left on America's moral and cultural landscape. The harsh reality is that if there is a pullout of Bible-believing evangelicals from the public square, America *will* still continue to have its public policy influenced by "spirituality." Unfortunately, that influence will bear little resemblance to the Judeo-Christian values that have served our nation well for the first two centuries of our national life. If unopposed, the message of the Dyers and the Chopras will help create a new moral consensus in America. That new moral consensus will be built on the mystical and mushy properties of spiritual self-fulfillment and personal inner enlightenment rather than on God's economy of revealed truth. That distorted moral compass, which directs the people of our republic, will in turn calibrate the direction of our ship of state. It promises the mirage of a safe harbor. But it will, in fact, send our nation into hidden and deadly reefs.

The extreme religious left has a firm coalition of alliances but has deftly avoided the appearance of organizational structure. It does not pronounce itself a "movement" (in fact, it disavows that description). It has, perhaps for those reasons, and perhaps because of the ideological affinity of many of those who control the mainstream press, escaped detection. It has certainly escaped the media's critical evaluation. On the other hand, there has been a consistent, lopsided attack against the religious right. This dichotomy makes the involvement of Bible-believing Christians even more urgent.

THE VILIFICATION OF THE RELIGIOUS RIGHT

Bill Clinton presents one of the best illustrations of this dichotomy in media treatment between Christian conservatives and the religious left. You will not find the mainstream media evaluating the impact of the religious left in providing political and moral cover for President Clinton. Rather, you will see the media benignly and gently referring to "spiritual advisers" who have "counseled" Bill Clinton. When his sexual misadventures with a White House intern were finally revealed, Clinton quickly surrounded himself with such "clergy."

For some time the two of us, during Bill Clinton's two terms as president, have been waiting (alas, in vain) for a newspaper headline that reads: "Clinton solicits support of religious liberals."

What we did get, however (and this from a conservative, mainstream newspaper) was a headline that read: "Clinton lashes out at religious conservatives."[2]

The reporting on Bill Clinton was accurate, of course. He did lash out at Christian conservatives in an interview with St. Louis radio station KMOX. The 1994 interview came on the heels of vitriolic attacks by Democrats against religious conservatives. Here was a prime example of conservative Christianity being tied to the whipping post while America watched the spectacle.

The question was not whether it was a deserved attack. The only question was how many lashes would be meted out.

Representative Vic Fazio, a Democrat from California, charged that Christian conservatives were part of a "radical" and "intolerant" fringe force attempting to take over the Republican Party. He mentioned Jerry Falwell and Pat Robertson by name.[3] Then Surgeon General Joycelyn Elders stoked the fires by ripping into what she described as the "un-Christian religious right" in a New York speech to the Lesbian and Gay Health Conference.

Eighty-seven House Republicans responded by asking President Clinton to fire Elders; forty-four Senate Republicans urged Bill Clinton to repudiate the Democratic attacks against conservative Christians. The president did indeed respond. However, in his response, he not only failed to repudiate this anti-Christian hate speech from his own minions, but he jumped into the fray in his radio interview, lambasting the religious "radical right" and complaining about the media power of religious conservatives who "have their own press organs" and who "make their own news." We couldn't help but think that he was attacking conservative talk show hosts in particular. We also couldn't help but think of the influence that, through God's blessings, *Janet Parshall's America* has had from the nation's capital across America. Yet there is always the attempt by Beltway liberals to slam-dunk the program as part of the "radical right."

Evangelical conservatives constantly find themselves having to stave off the kind of attacks that lump them into the "shadowy and sinister religious right wing." In tune with the remarks of Bill Clinton, author David Frum wrote an op-ed in *USA Today* entitled "Myth of the Religious Right."[4] His premise was not merely that the religious right was bad for America (he called Ollie North and other conservatives "sinister" and "self-seeking demagogues"); rather, he concluded that Christian conservative voices were really very inconsequential. The religious right, he apparently believes, is actually quite powerless. Yet he also wrote, without hesitation, that it is inherently evil.

In recent times Hillary Clinton has tried to make political capital out of the sinister characterization of religious conservatives. She even went so far as to attribute the Independent Counsel's investigation into her husband to a "vast right-wing conspiracy."

The "religious right" label has been around for at least two decades. It has been a handy way to pigeonhole (and demonize) evangelical Christians who become active in public affairs. The two of us have read countless fund-raising letters, public relations memos, and press releases from organizations dedicated to opposing, tooth and nail, the efforts of Christian conservatives. Organizations like the American Civil Liberties Union (ACLU), Americans United for Separation of Church and State, and People for the American Way regularly paint a ghoulish picture of the religious right wing.

Moreover, the obvious anti-Christian bias of the mainstream media now seems established beyond debate. Three professors of political science at three major secular universities (University of Wisconsin, University of Oklahoma, and Clemson University) arrived at this opinion after carefully researching the subject. They concluded that "one of the greatest impediments to Christian Right success has been the hostility of the elite media. There is no question that leading print and television news sources have been decidedly negative toward the Religious Right. Once they discovered its existence in 1980, they began to attack it—and they continue to do so today."[5]

Yet this war of words waged against Christians has not been limited to national politics. The chances are very good that your local school board, your local PTA, or some of your public school administrators have received literature on how to combat evangelical Christians.

Materials we have collected over the years include *Challenging the Christian Right* (courtesy of the National Education Association), which contains a state-by-state description of right-wing organizations to watch out for, including Focus on the Family, the Christian Coalition, Concerned Women for America, and the American Family Association. Another favorite is *If You Don't, They Will—A Political Guide for Successful School Support*, a workbook designed to equip educators and community members to resist groups like the National Association of Christian Educators. ("Be aware that your opponents will bring in video recorders and tape recorders to board meetings and other functions. They'll also come equipped with notebooks and look like they're taking everybody's name. Do the same thing, while smiling serenely. It drives them nuts."[6]) Lastly, there is the *National PTA's Guide to Extremism—Extremists—Extremist Groups* (i.e., almost anyone who objects to the content of a book in the library, or anyone who objects to any public school curriculum).

The two of us had an interesting experience that illustrates how conservative Christians have been targeted. We first began our foray into the process of applying our gospel beliefs into social and public policy issues quite unexpectedly. It all started when we stumbled across some of the startling things going on in our own neighborhood public education system. We had both grown up attending the same midwestern grade school and high school. Janet later taught, as an elementary music teacher, in this same system. We also enrolled our then-small children in that public school district.

Then one day one of our elementary-grade daughters came home and shared a confusing experience. She had been in her class at school when the teacher put all of the students in a circle. The children, all under ten years old, were asked to share very personal and private feelings about a variety of topics that seemed to have nothing to do with the curriculum. The children were asked about any upsetting experiences in their homes. They were asked, for example, what would happen if there were a divorce: how would they feel about that, and which parent did they think they would rather live with?

We approached the teacher believing, naively, that there had been some mistake in this highly questionable exercise. What we discovered is that this was the tip of the iceberg. We discovered that our school district, like many others around the nation, was experimenting in a mandatory, in-class developmental guidance program. The program raised immense privacy issues because it delved into areas that violated the privacy of parents and children. It also raised legal issues because it was being administered without the prior informed consent of the parents. The program, which had a startling similarity to the client-based therapy techniques of psychotherapy pioneer Carl Rogers, also raised ethical concerns: the children were not patients, and the adult discussion leaders were not licensed psychologists.

When we pressed our concerns, we were summoned before an informal tribunal of school administrators. One of the administration officials started off the meeting something like this: "Now, we are here today to address some of your concerns about our developmental guidance program. But first we have something we have to ask you."

At this point we expected a few questions about our children's class, and the nature of our complaint. Instead he continued:

"We need to know—are you here today because you are opposed to secular humanism?"

What was significant about that question was the fact that neither of us had mentioned any concerns over secular humanism (or anything close to that).

"What do you mean by 'secular humanism'?" we asked.

"Well . . ." The administrator paused and then said sheepishly, "I'm really not sure."

"Well, if you are not sure, then what difference does it make whether I'm for or against it?" Janet responded in her best classroom-teacher voice. After an embarrassed silence, the group finally came around to actually discussing a few of our concerns. It was clear, however, that these public school officials had been forewarned about the "right-wing Christians" who were about to do battle in their schools over something called "secular humanism" (even though the school officials could not quite define what that was).

As we further researched some of these controversial and troublesome trends in the public schools, we discovered an immense wealth of evidence that the public schools were being educated and trained, at great expense of time and money, to do battle with what they perceived as right-wing religious zealots. The cover of one particular professional educational journal at that time comes to mind. On the cover was the cartoon of a clown, with a particularly demented smile, ripping out the pages of a textbook in a crazed frenzy. The title said: "Get the clowns out of your curriculum." The point of the cover was made quite clear by the context of the article inside: we conservative evangelicals who were beginning to complain about what our children were being taught were the clowns.

Our experience in these issues, over the course of many years, has proven to us that there has been a concerted effort to demonize, and then marginalize, evangelical conservatives when it comes to the important issues of the day. Religious liberals, on the other hand, have been given a free pass to influence public issues without being hampered by labels, epithets, or mischaracterization.

Yet it is essential to understand that religious liberalism, and its influence on our culture and public policy, is not limited to people who overtly reject the Christian message. There is a mounting challenge within evangelicalism that calls for our reasoned and energetic response.

THE EVANGELICAL SOLDIERS OF THE RELIGIOUS LEFT

More than a decade ago Francis Schaeffer noted:

> If it is fair to talk of "The New Right" and the religious "Right Wing," then it must be equally fair to speak of the religious "Left Wing"—concerning those within evangelicalism who have accommodated to the dominant form of the world spirit of our day.[7]

Schaeffer was slow to use labels like "right wing" or "left wing." But he also admitted that the label "religious left" was a fair one to use in addressing the problems of the liberal evangelicals who accommodate the ideas of the world in their thinking, in their actions, and in the way they attempt to solve social problems.

The power and organization of the religious left ought, in itself, to be a strong motivation for traditional evangelicals not to retreat. More disturbing is the fact that much of the religious left flexes its muscle not only from what it describes as a Christian position, but even from an evangelical position.

Theologian Walter Wink, for example, has been described as a scholar whose "theology is shaped as much by his study of the Bible as by his involvement in the civil rights movement and the fight against apartheid in South Africa," and who "helps us reformulate our 'ancient religious concepts'—such as God and Satan."[8] Wink, formerly of the Union Theological Seminary, probably qualifies, as much as anyone, for membership in the religious left.

How does he characterize the religious right? To Walter Wink, evangelicals like Jerry Falwell and Pat Robertson are merely "champions of the warrior mentality" in matters of American policy. Wink makes the astonishing conclusion that "applying Jesus' way of creative nonviolence to political situations is for them indistinguishable from cowardice."[9] For those of us who know and have worked alongside these two gentlemen, this kind of gross and outlandish character assassination requires a loving and persistent advocacy of what evangelicals *really* stand for. Retreat from these kinds of misrepresentations would only create the irony of the "heckler's veto" for evangelicals—where the intellectual hecklers in the culture are given the right to mischaracterize and harass us into abject silence.

In direct response to the activities of such groups as the Moral Majority and the Christian Coalition, a movement of religious liberals has gained prominence. Chief among those of this new countermovement is Jim Wallis. Wallis came from a Plymouth Brethren background and attended Trinity Evangelical Divinity School, a school known for its evangelical orthodoxy. Yet his social and political positions caused an uproar among the faculty and alumni when he organized antiwar protests on campus.[10]

Wallis pioneered a new magazine, *Sojourners*, and spearheaded an attempt to redefine 1990s evangelicalism in the fashion of 1960s radicalism.

For Wallis, the position of these *new evangelicals* is not a matter of religious right or religious left—or even a matter of conservative versus liberal. He seeks a "new politics of community" based on a "radical" view of Jesus and a social program that transcends the traditional labels. Yet under close analysis, the *Sojourners* movement looks and sounds like Norman Lear's People for the American Way with a coat of theology brushed over it.

According to *Sojourners,* those of us who are part of the pro-family religious right are engaged in a public debate that is increasingly "divisive, intolerant, and partisan."[11] We have "hijacked American evangelicalism."[12]

There is no question that adherents of the *Sojourners* movement consider themselves evangelical. In one publication seven articles are devoted to the question "What is Evangelical?"[13] Yet in their attempt to portray themselves as the third way of enlightenment and therefore somehow different from the old arguments about the Right and the Left of American culture, something does not ring true.

Take, for instance, Jim Wallis's critique—which we are sure was intended to be evenhanded—of the problems with both the religious right and the religious left.

As for the religious liberals, Wallis offers only two rather soft-spoken, throat-clearing asides: First, he reminds us that "liberal activism has often lacked any real dynamic of personal conversion." Translated, this means that theological liberals have looked to bettering the world rather than saving souls. Second, he states that when Protestant liberal leaders gained access to the White House, they tended to "tone down" their moral indictments against the president and his administration.[14]

But when it comes time for Wallis to lay into the religious

right, blood splatters and fur flies. Here are just a few of his epithets: We [conservative evangelicals or fundamentalists] have
created a "false religion" by fostering "a bizarre and frightening
combination of religion and politics." We have "become preoccupied with words and dogma." We have further polarized "an
already divided and polarized society." We have propagated "a
white religion." We have "fueled the backlash against women's
rights," and we have "used blatant caricatures and attacks on
homosexuals." We have created an "unholy alliance of religious
appeals and right-wing politics." And last, but certainly not
least, we have "produced a gospel of prosperity" at home while
being a "consistent defender of the nation's every war" abroad.[15]

Clearly, what Wallis and company are selling is just a repack-
aged version of the same tired attacks against the cultural influence of born-again Christians we have heard before. Their
publication is rife with frontal offensives against such familiar
targets as the Christian Coalition (and the supposed danger of
its insider access to Washington) and Pat Robertson (he is
accused of blurring the lines between money and politics). This
rhetoric has been used before by such groups as the National
Organization for Women, the ACLU, People for the American
Way, Planned Parenthood, Americans United for the Separation
of Church and State, and the National Education Association,
to name just a few from the familiar list of usual suspects.

One of the major coalitions of the religious left is the Interfaith Alliance. That organization was born out of a desire to
combat what they felt was an unfair public perception that such
organizations as the Christian Coalition spoke for all people of
faith. The Alliance is quick to join with Jim Wallis in condemning the religious right.

C. Welton Gaddy, a Baptist minister and executive director of the Interfaith Alliance, is described as someone who has devoted his energies to religious "pluralism and challenging extremism."[16] Gaddy contends that "the Religious Right often perpetuate[s] stereotypes that create a false dichotomy between religiously conservative Republicans and secular, liberal Democrats."[17]

Sister Mary Carol Bennett, a board member of the southwestern Pennsylvania chapter of the Alliance, complains about "the Religious Right's manipulation of religious language and symbols" in a supposed campaign that results in a "disconnect between rhetoric and reality" in matters of religious values and public policy.[18]

The Interfaith Alliance has unveiled, in time for the upcoming presidential election, its new project, called "Call to a Faithful Decision 2000." This program seeks to influence "people of faith and their faith communities" in time for the national elections. It has wasted no time in criticizing, as an example, George W. Bush, who has supported a voucher system for private religious schools, and who has supported the ability of students and citizens to express their religious beliefs. The Alliance has suggested that somehow his personal expression of Christian faith is necessarily inconsistent with his support for the death penalty.[19]

What is significantly different about the approaches of *Sojourners* and the Interfaith Alliance is that in the midst of their campaign against the religious right, they are seeking to redefine, for evangelicals, what evangelicalism *is*. They are also defining, when it comes to social action, what evangelicalism *is not*.

It is wrong to assume that this struggle for self-definition within evangelicalism is limited merely to issues of social action or influence on the political process. We are in the midst of a great struggle to define and direct the future of evangelicalism on the most basic concepts of faith and practice. There is even a beginning of a polar shift within the evangelical Church on such basic theological issues as the nature of personal salvation and whether salvation is available by means other than through Christ alone. Prominent evangelical theologian Clark Pinnock, along with several others, has suggested that salvation is available to some through a general revelation of God's grace, rather than through faith in the specific revelation of Jesus Christ as God's atoning sacrifice.[20]

This theological thunderstorm has been brewing for most of the 1990s. How the dispute over this fundamental biblical tenet has currently sparked lightning bolts in the public policy arena was illustrated in a debate between Jerry Falwell and Tony Campolo on *Crossfire*. While debating issues of religion and politics, Campolo was asked to clarify his position on salvation by faith in Christ. His response clearly created the impression that, like Clark Pinnock, Tony Campolo (who consistently calls himself an evangelical) subscribes to inclusivism, the tenet that God's grace is available to save, in some circumstances, without profession of faith in the sacrificial work of Christ on the cross. Many of us who consider ourselves evangelical/fundamentalist in our theology winced at Mr. Campolo's pronouncement.

A hundred years ago the great London preacher Charles Spurgeon remarked that it does little good to cry out against the apostasy of the day with the plea that "we are evangelicals," if we lack the courage to declare what being evangelical *really means*. When the gospel is twisted and used as political cover for vicious attacks on the Church of Jesus Christ, a cry of protest from the Church is necessary. This is part of the prophetic role of the saved, sanctified, and spiritually energized Church. Sometimes it will require us to denounce those who seek to speak for the Lord but communicate a corrupted message: "How can you say, 'We are wise, / And the law of the LORD is with us?' / But behold, the lying pen of the scribes / Has made it into a lie" (Jer. 8:8).

This is not about defending our names, our ministries, or even the conservative evangelical movement. It is about refusing to be silenced when our communities, our nation, and our sin-sick world are most in need of hearing and seeing a demonstration of the *whole truth* of the *whole gospel.* We must do this truthfully and yet lovingly. But it must be done—and it must be done now, sooner rather than later.

In order to undertake that great task, then, a great opportunity of self-definition for Bible-believing Christians is now at hand. We must define, upon the authority of Scripture and guided by the Holy Spirit, *what it means* to be saved, and *by what means* we are saved, and what that salvation *means for us* in His service, as salt and light to the world.

3

Saints and Sinners in Society: Bible Figures Who Impacted Their Cultures

ANYONE WHO IS under the mistaken assumption that God's people are called to disengage from their culture needs a primer in Bible history. From the Old Testament to the New Testament, examples abound of how the children of God have successfully influenced their communities, their cultures, and their governments. The following are just a few biblical examples.

TENT PEGS, PALM TREES, AND THE WOMEN OF GOD

First, we need to go back to around 1360 B.C. The nation of Israel, under the leadership of Joshua and following God's directive, had conquered most of the land of Canaan, although a few Canaanite strongholds remained to battle the individual Israelite tribes. The nation had enjoyed the benefits of Joshua's inspired campaign as the commander in chief of the Lord's army as he led Israel's military advance into the land God had given them. By the time of the battles described in the book of Joshua, the culture of Canaan had become a full-fledged moral and spiritual abomination. God waited some four hundred years until

Canaan's evil was "complete" (Gen. 15:16) before bringing it under His judgment, through the sword of Israel.

But now Joshua was dead, and Israel faced a crisis—not only in leadership, but also a crisis of the spirit. The land still contained remnants of the enemies of God and their pagan practices. The work to which Joshua had been called now needed to be completed. Before his death, Joshua had challenged the people to make a pledge of obedience to the Lord: "Now therefore, put away the foreign gods which are in your midst, and incline your hearts to the LORD, the God of Israel" (Josh. 24:23).

The people accepted this pledge, and their covenant with the Lord was inscribed on a stone in a public place, as a constant reminder (Josh. 24:24–27).

However, following Joshua's death, the majority of the tribes of Israel failed to drive the enemies out of their land. They also failed to make good on their covenant with God (Judg. 1:19–36). As a result, because they did not fully tear down the pagan altars and drive them out, God declared that the Canaanites "shall become as thorns in your sides, and their gods shall be a snare to you" (Judg. 2:3).

At first the children of God merely permitted the practice of pagan worship to continue in their midst. But slowly they began to absorb these detestable and heretical forms of worship into their own spiritual practices. Before long they "did what was evil in the sight of the LORD, and forgot the LORD their God, and served the Baals and the Asheroth" (Judg. 3:7).

Baal was a particularly revered pagan god. His name, in ancient Ugaritic, meant *lord* or *owner*. His appeal was his supposed control over the power of rain or drought; therefore, he was thought to possess the power to bestow great material prosperity or sudden financial collapse. As the Church enters the twenty-first century, we ought to wonder whether, in the lap of American luxury, we have allowed a subtle but modern version of Baal worship to seep into our worldview.

Asheroth was the ancient goddess of both love and war, and was invoked to justify unspeakable acts of violence. It is interesting that our current society, which consistently declares its pursuit of "love," has become, at the same time, the most violent nation on earth. In ancient Israel, these two false deities—Baal and Asheroth—were worshipped in Canaanite culture with acts of male and female temple prostitution and even human sacrifice. Before we condemn the ancient children of Israel too quickly for their tolerance of such practices, we ought to take a hard look at our own attitudes toward sexual promiscuity and the slaughter of preborn human life.

As the ancient people of God engaged in pagan marriages and absorbed idolatry into their culture, they began to realize that, along with this form of syncretism and compromise, they were also becoming oppressed by the Canaanites. Faced with the bitter result of their spiritual betrayal, they "cried to the LORD" (Judg. 3:9). God answered by giving them a series of "judges" who were led by the Spirit of the Lord. These judges were commissioned by God to provide moral and military deliverance as well as practical leadership.

We find one of those judges, Deborah, sitting under a palm tree on the hills overlooking ancient Ephraim. It was there that God gave Deborah the message that Barak, one of Israel's military leaders, was to engage the occupying Canaanite army at Mount Tabor. Victory was guaranteed by the Lord (Judg. 4:7). But to Barak's shame, he was reluctant to follow God's directive when Deborah announced it to him. It was only after Deborah had agreed to personally escort Barak and his troops into battle that he agreed to obey his heavenly orders.

As He had promised, God routed the Canaanite troops in the wake of Barak's attack and sent their general, Sisera, running for his life. Deborah, as a leader of her nation, had helped to fulfill the work left undone with the death of Joshua.

The enemy commander, madly trying to escape the pursuing army of Israel, made his way to one of the Israelite tribes that had previously maintained peaceful relations with the Canaanites. Sisera obviously thought he could find sanctuary with that group. But there, in that tribe, minding her own business in the midst of a military cataclysm, was Jael, a wife who was tending to her tent. Sisera had no idea he was about to meet one of Israel's great patriots.

Jael obviously knew what to do. In an exercise of skillful counterintelligence, she coaxed the desperate and fatigued Sisera into her tent. She covered him with a rug so he could get cozy for a nice nap, and she even gave him a bottle of milk to help him nod off. Then, when he was fast asleep, Jael took the implements of her own household—a hammer and a tent peg—and drove the peg into the head of this sleeping enemy officer with such force that he became fastened tight to the ground (Judg. 4:21).

By the time Barak arrived on the scene with his Israelite troops, there was nothing left to do except celebrate. The battle became the turning point in defeating the king of Canaan. We are told that "the land was undisturbed for forty years" as a result of that battle (Judg. 5:31).

The story of this great battle at Tabor illustrates how God brought national victory through the very different, but equally important, contributions of women. Women of God can serve the Lord wherever they are. You may be called to a position of leadership in the front lines of the cultural and spiritual battles of the twenty-first century. There may be a palm tree and some great battle in your future. If you are a Deborah, take heed to the song that beckons you. You are enouraged to "Awake, awake, Deborah; / Awake, awake, sing a song!" (Judg. 5:12). Be bold both to do great works in His power, and to declare the praises of our great and awesome Lord.

You may be a woman who is called to serve the Lord in your tent and your household. If you are, then Jael has a message for you. With the common implements of faithfulness in your home, you can help drive a stake through evil without even leaving the front step. "Most blessed of women is Jael, / The wife of Heber the Kenite; / Most blessed is she of women in the tent," we are told in Judges 5:24. Through your godly influence on your children and your household, through your courage to oppose all things opposed to the Lord, and through your willingness to do His bidding, you, too, can be "most blessed . . . of women in the tent!"

REBUILDING THE CHURCH WALLS AND PETITIONING IN THE STATE HALLS

Another great lesson is to be learned in the rebuilding of the ancient temple in Jerusalem. That story nicely illustrates how God's people can protect the walls of their right to worship by the joint venture of spiritual leadership, practical effort, and skillful dealings with a hostile government.

In 586 B.C. one of the great blows to Jewish national identity and worship occurred. Babylon had dominated that part of the world, but plans for revolt had been laid among Jewish leaders who were trying to create a coalition of military support with Egypt. King Nebuchadnezzar of Babylon set his mind to put down the revolt with such ferocity that Israel would never rise again. In 588 B.C. he sent his army to Jerusalem. A violent siege of that city went on for two years, until it finally fell to the Babylonians. The great Temple of Solomon, the center of Jewish sacrifice and worship, was utterly destroyed. Zedekiah, the Jewish king of the revolting Judean forces, was captured, and he was cruelly made to watch the execution of his two sons before the Babylonians put out his eyes.

About fifty years later, however, Cyrus and his Persian Empire defeated the Babylonians. Cyrus was considerably more humane than his vicious predecessor. Archaeological discoveries have revealed that he believed in a general policy of resettlement of the Jewish citizens to the places from which they had been displaced. In the first year of his reign, Cyrus issued a remarkable decree permitting the Jewish people in Babylon to return to Jerusalem and rebuild their destroyed temple. The decree even instructed the citizens to give a "freewill offering for the house of God which is in Jerusalem" (Ezra 1:4).

We are reminded, of course, that the heart of every king is ultimately in the hands of the Lord. In this case, "the Lord stirred up the spirit of Cyrus king of Persia" (Ezra 1:1) to permit the rebuilding of the great temple and thus fulfill the prophecy made two hundred years earlier by the prophet Isaiah (chaps. 44–45). Construction of the temple began, and with the laying of its foundation there was great joy and thanksgiving by a people that had long been displaced, persecuted, and demoralized (Ezra 3:11).

Zerubbabel, who as part of the Davidic line (Matt. 1:12) was in succession to be king of Judea, was appointed by Cyrus as governor over Jerusalem. Zerubbabel took the leadership position of overseeing the rebuilding of the temple. But whenever the work of God is undertaken, opposition soon follows. Enemies of the rebuilding effort arose among the non-Jewish citizens of Judea.

Their first strategy was a clever one: they would offer to assist with the project and seek to sabotage it from the inside (Ezra 4:2). But Zerubbabel was shrewd enough politically, and wise enough spiritually, to understand one of the basic rules of coalitions: Don't bother coalescing with those with whom you have differences so fundamentally and diametrically opposed that your mission will be frustrated. Zerubbabel declared: "You have nothing in common with us in building a house to our God" (Ezra 4:3).

Undaunted, the opponents of the project pulled out the big guns and hired some high-powered lawyers ("counselors" with some "pull" at the palace). Their purpose was to discourage, frustrate, and frighten the people of God from pursuing their grant of religious liberties (Ezra 4:4–5).

They pleaded their cause with the new king, Ahasuerus (Xerxes I), and later to King Artaxerxes in a written plea so full of craft and distortion that it would give even the most hardened litigator the chills. For instance, they argued that the Jews were actually attempting to rebuild the entire *city* of Jerusalem (Ezra 4:12). This was blatantly false, of course, as their project dealt only with the temple itself, not the entire city. Then, for good measure, the opponents argued that this whole effort smacked of rebellion: "They are rebuilding the rebellious and evil city . . . they have incited revolt within it in past days" (Ezra 4:12, 15).

But the next argument is a familiar one, even now, twenty-five hundred years later. When in doubt, attack the church project as something that will drain the public treasury because of tax exemptions: "They will not pay tribute, custom or toll, and it will damage the revenue of the kings" (Ezra 4:13).

The last appeal amounts to mere pandering to the honor of the king. The dissenters contended that *they* (unlike the Jewish settlers) "are in the service of the palace, and it is not fitting for us to see the king's dishonor" by the actions of these religious zealots (Ezra 4:14).

Unfortunately, this legal maneuver was successful in delaying the building of the temple. The king granted a temporary restraining order against the project until further order (Ezra 4:21), and work stopped for some fifteen years.

The people of God were now faced with two competing legal documents. The first was a decree from King Cyrus granting them full faith and credit in the rebuilding of their temple and the reinstitution of their religious practices. The second decree, actually issued in apparent ignorance of the first decree (through the sly legal tactics of the anti-Jewish opponents), ordered the project to a halt until further notice.

Then two prophets, Haggai and Zechariah, came onto the scene. They became the exhorters who would motivate Zerubbabel to resume work on the temple, in opposition to the order of King Artaxerxes (Ezra 5:1). It is essential to note that more than just political leadership was needed here. Spiritual leadership was also a necessary component. We are told that while Zerubbabel and his staff commenced the rebuilding effort, "the prophets of God were with them supporting them" (Ezra 5:2).

Then a second wave of opposition arose, this time from Tattenai, the pagan governor of the area. After sending his inspectors to the site to find out the names of those responsible for the resumption of construction, he wrote to the king, now Darius I, complaining about the building effort (Ezra 5:7–10). With his appeal he also filed the reply of the Jews, which argued, as a legal basis for the project, that the prior decree of King Cyrus had authorized the building of the temple.

Tattenai asked for a ruling from King Darius. He received

one, but it was not the ruling he expected. The decision of the king was a grand-slam home run for Zerubbabel and his Jewish supporters. King Darius not only affirmed the right to rebuild the temple, but he also ordered that the tax revenues of Tattenai's own province be used to help fund the project! (Ezra 6:7–8)

Six years into the reign of King Darius, the temple was finally completed. But without the final contribution of effort by one of God's chosen men, that huge and controversial undertaking would have been mere shine and polish, with no spiritual substance. For that purpose the Lord raised up Ezra, a scribe trained in the law of God. Ezra was able to skillfully negotiate the assistance of the king, who permitted the transportation of the large staff of priests, temple workers, and others who would actually oversee the running of the temple. "The king granted him all he requested because the hand of the LORD his God was upon him" (Ezra 7:6). Ezra was also successful in receiving a decree from the king that permitted the full exercise of religious liberties in the temple and even included the exemption of the temple workers from taxation (Ezra 7:24).

The remaining portion of the book of Ezra tells of the righteous example set by Ezra as the spiritual leader of the people, and the revolutionary effect of his absolute insistence on the teaching of, and obedience to, the Word of God.

Through the contributions of men gifted in biblical exhortation, political administration and negotiation, and the teaching and modeling of scriptural truth, God's people were protected, worship of the Lord was promoted, and the national nightmare of pagan occupation and near decimation was ended.

But the challenges to the people of God were not over. An even greater threat still had to be faced. This time they would be spared because of the help of a godly queen.

FOR SUCH A TIME AS THIS

The son of King Darius I was Xerxes I (the Bible calls him Ahasuerus), who ruled much of the Middle East after him. The Persian Empire exercised the power of occupation over the Jews, but hostilities were at a minimum. However, in the world of palace intrigue, being close to the king could be a curse—or a source of miraculous blessing.

Xerxes had a queen, named Vashti, who was a stunning beauty. One day Xerxes, who had been on a seven-day drinking binge with his noblemen, suddenly got the urge to show off his trophy queen to his princes. So he ordered her to make an immediate appearance before him in full regalia—crown, jewels, and all. Vashti refused. The book of Esther records that Vashti was quickly, and not surprisingly, deposed by the king and stripped of her crown (Est. 1:19). She was banished from the king's presence. Xerxes may have later realized that his demand to parade his wife before his nobles was inappropriate; he was in a drunken state at the time. Or perhaps her name (Vashti means *best*) gives us a hint of the special place she held in his harem of wives. In any event, though he possessed the authority to have her executed, the king did not do so.

What the king did do, however, in a burst of chauvinistic bravado, was to issue a silly and unenforceable decree that must have thrilled henpecked husbands everywhere. He proclaimed that every man in the kingdom should henceforth be lord and master over his wife! (Est. 1:21–22). It was not long, though, before the king began regretting his banishment of the beautiful Vashti. His counselors, quick to appease the king's longing for his chief wife, suggested a kind of royal beauty contest among the best-looking virgins in the land. In the capital city of Susa lived a fellow named Mordecai, who was a Jew and a gatekeeper of the palace. He lived there with his young cousin Esther, whom he had adopted and raised as his daughter. She is described as "beautiful of form and face " (Est. 2:7). Esther was rounded up with the other beautiful virgins of the kingdom and taken to the palace, where she spent an entire year in preparation for her presentation to the king.

When the time came, Esther, who possessed not only physical beauty but also a gracious and kind spirit, won the king's heart. She was crowned queen, taking the honored place of Vashti. In God's sovereignty, there are no accidents. In His economy, no position, talent, or experience is ever wasted.

Following the installation of Esther as queen, we see the rise to power in King Xerxes' court of a wicked man named Haman. Haman was the kind of power-hungry bureaucrat who reveled in making people grovel before him. When Mordecai refused to bow down before him, Haman was enraged. His cronies advised Haman that this Mordecai was a Jew. Armed with that information, Haman set upon a perverse plan for ultimate revenge. He would destroy not just Mordecai and his family. He would, instead, exterminate the entire Jewish population in the occupied kingdom.

Haman skillfully presented this matter to the king as a problem of unruly foreigners. As he explained, there were a "certain people" in the kingdom (he did not say that they were Jews) whose "laws are different" and who "do not observe the king's laws" (Est. 3:8). Haman requested, and received, the king's authority to destroy them. The king was so successfully manipulated by Haman that he gave his royal signet ring to authenticate the death warrant, and he then permitted Haman to draft and seal his own decree, sight unseen. Haman distributed copies of the extermination orders to all of the provinces, and set a certain date for all of the executions to take place and for the seizure of all Jewish assets as plunder.

But God would not permit His people to be utterly destroyed. This was similar to the situation that would face the early church some five hundred years later. A certain anti-Christian zealot by the name of Saul of Tarsus was taking a similar decree in hand to the city of Damascus. Saul's decree permitted him to arrest, and probably even execute, any Christians he found in that city. In both cases God intervened. In the case of Saul, God's Son miraculously appeared before him on the road and stopped his malicious plan by bringing about Saul's confession of Jesus as Lord and changing his heart. But in the case of Haman, it was apparently a heart so hardened that it would not be turned. So God intervened in a different way—through Queen Esther.

Mordecai, who had access to the latest palace gossip, became aware of Haman's plot. He immediately contacted his adopted daughter through a messenger and urged her to plead with the king to reverse the extermination order. At first Esther was understandably reluctant. The king had not summoned her to appear before him in a month. It was the law of the land that any person who appeared in the presence of the king without a specific royal invitation would be put to death. And that sentence of execution could only be reversed if the king chose to show mercy by extending his golden scepter to the unfortunate person. Esther knew that to appear before the king without a request from him would mean almost certain death.

But Mordecai prevailed upon Esther to realize her place in God's plan. It was no accident, he said, that she had been ushered into a position of influence to the most powerful man in the known world. He came right to the point: "For if you remain silent at this time, relief and deliverance will arise for the Jews from another place and you and your father's house will perish. And who knows whether you have not attained royalty for such a time as this?" (Est. 4:14).

Esther was convinced. She asked Mordecai to assemble every Jewish believer in the city and urge them to fast before the Lord, to aid her in her task. "I will go in to the king, which is not according to the law," Esther said, "and if I perish, I perish" (Est. 4:16).

She did not perish, of course, because in fact, she *had* attained royalty for such a time as exactly that. And when she was able, with impressive discretion, to reveal Haman's dastardly plan, Xerxes turned on his scheming lieutenant with white-hot rage. Haman had been so confident in his conspiracy that he had built a seventy-five-foot gallows and intended to personally oversee the execution of Mordecai. That very execution device would be used, but for quite a different purpose. Xerxes ordered Haman to be hung on his own gallows. But the king's reaction—and God's blessing—did not end there. Mordecai, who had secretly foiled an earlier assassination attempt on the king but had not received the credit, was honored and elevated in the kingdom. Xerxes issued an official proclamation granting the Jews in his kingdom the fullest power of assembly and of self-defense against anyone who would threaten their existence.

The gracious and fair Esther, who had started out as just one more young Jewish girl in a hostile land, had been obedient to the Lord. As a result, she gained access to the corridors of political power and ended up saving the people of God from annihilation.

THE PROPHET WHO CHALLENGED A NATION

Is it ever appropriate for those of us in "the Lord's army" to raise voices of protest against the ruling powers of our country?

If you have any doubts about that, come and meet John the Baptist. He was a wild and woolly kind of fellow. The Bible says that he wore a leather belt and a cloak made of camel's hair, and he survived on the locusts and wild honey in the Judean wilderness (Matt. 3:4).

When we think of the refined and polite meetings in Washington, D.C. that Christian groups often sponsor, we wonder how this "rough around the edges" character would be received. Would we take a second or third look at his ragged appearance? Would we wince at his clear, bold, no-holds-barred approach to truth? And if we knew he intended to walk over the white marble buildings in the South Capitol Street area publicly denouncing the Congress, and then cross the street to the Supreme Court building so he could take on the black-robed justices, would we try to talk some sense into him?

John was not a palace kind of man. His calling was not to minister in the midst of palatial splendor and courtly manners. Instead, his forum was the harsh and unforgiving stretch of desert along the western edge of the Dead Sea. When both of us had the thrill of first visiting that stark and lonely area of Israel a few years back, we could not help but think of this rugged "Baptizer" and prophet. We thought of the tough, gritty life he led in the furnacelike heat of the desert, in that land of limestone and sand—a landscape that more resembles the forbidden surface of the moon than the earth.

John was the last of the Old Testament prophets. After a four-hundred-year silence between the Old and New Testaments, suddenly, out of the forbidding wilderness, John the Baptist burst onto the scene as God's prophet to herald the coming of the Messiah. Jesus remarked that John was the greatest prophet of them all (Matt. 11:11). As Bible scholar John F. Walvoord puts it, "Like the servants of a king who would smooth out and straighten the road in preparation for their sovereign's coming, so John was preparing the way spiritually for the coming of Christ.[1]

Yet what is fascinating to note is the content of this great messenger's message. John preached on three main themes: eschatological teaching (the imminent reality of the kingdom of heaven through the arrival of Christ, the Messiah); prophetic denunciation (the condemnation of immorality and spiritual bankruptcy when contrasted with God's Word); and ethical instruction.[2] Understandably, his main message was eschatological. But why the other themes as well? If you or I were told to be God's messenger, to "Make ready the way of the Lord, / Make His paths straight" (Mark 1:3), and we were led to preach the message that "the kingdom of God is at hand; repent and believe in the gospel" (Mark 1:15), would we have done it the way John did? And would we have been as political as he was?

"Political?" you ask. Yet, if we describe political action as any communication or pressure of persuasion brought to bear on those in civil authority in hopes of influencing their values and their decisions, then "political" is exactly what this desert prophet was.

Scripture describes three distinct governmental groups that John addressed. First, he addressed the tax collectors. Rome, like modern America, was rife with a variety of taxes. They had a poll tax on every male over fourteen years of age, and on every female over twelve. Only the very aged were exempt from taxes. There were land taxes and taxes on goods, including slaves. Imports and exports were taxed at toll booths and bridges. Tax collecting was, in fact, a handsomely profitable business. The tax collectors were like independent contractors who would collect and remit the taxes to the Roman government. But because they regularly overtaxed the beleaguered citizens, the tax collectors pocketed the excess as their profit.

One day some tax collectors came to the Jordan River to be baptized by John. "Teacher," they asked him, "what shall we do?" (Luke 3:12). John did not tell them to get out of the dirty business of consorting with the Roman government. Instead, he imparted the ethical rules that were applicable to their political office and in keeping with the kingdom principles he had been sent to preach. John simply instructed them, "Collect no more than what you have been ordered to" (Luke 3:13). John was saying, in effect, "If you are in a position of government authority, be honest."

At the same time John encountered a second group of government officials. The Bible says that soldiers came to him asking, "And what about us, what shall we do?" Soldiers were often brutal to the civilian population, and many times used their position of power to extort money. John's advice was plain: "Do not take money from anyone by force, or accuse anyone falsely, and be content with your wages" (Luke 3:14). John was saying that when you live by kingdom principles, you do not use the power of your official position to manipulate others, or to frustrate the machinery of justice, or to extort those who are subject to you.

Herod represented the third political target for John's preaching. The Gospels of Luke, Matthew, and Mark all record John's encounters with this tyrannical ruler. The Herodian dynasty was of Jewish lineage, yet they ruled ancient Israel as an arm of the Roman occupation.

In this family dynasty, Herod Antipas (4 B.C.–A.D. 39) was the tetrarch who ruled over Galilee during the ministries of John the

Baptist and Jesus of Nazareth. In the house of Herod, the sons learned to be ruthless in their pursuit of power and civil authority. The father of Herod Antipas was Herod the Great, who had mercilessly murdered all of the male infants in Bethlehem rather than risk the possibility that his position would be rivaled by the prophesied Messiah.

The supporters of the dynasty's rule in Israel were called Herodians in Scripture. Nothing good is said of either Herod or his followers in the Bible. Herod Antipas, at the urging of his wife, had John the Baptist executed. Herod and his loyalists also conspired with the Pharisees to destroy Jesus. This conspiracy seems to have taken root at the earliest stages of Jesus' ministry (Mark 3:6). The Bible on occasion describes sympathetic members of the Pharisees—Joseph of Arimathea, for example, as well as Nicodemus, and even unnamed Pharisees who warned Jesus of Herod's plot to kill Him (Luke 13:31). But there are no positive references to either Herod or his political cronies in the Bible.[3]

Herod's chief talent was apparently his political craftiness and deceit. Jesus referred to him as "that fox" (Luke 13:32). Herod's chief ambition, like any godless politician, was to insure his power base. It is no accident that when his supporters, together with the Pharisees, tried (in vain) to trap Jesus into taking a damaging position, they chose as their debating point the matter of taxes (Mark 12:13–15). The issue of taxes was of vital importance to the continued power of the Roman state and to Herod, its provincial puppet. In the typical spirit of political gamesmanship, Herod was able to put aside past conflicts with Pontius Pilate, the Roman governor in Judea. Herod forged a temporary alliance with Pilate at the time of the trial of Jesus (Luke 23:12).

John the Baptist did not hesitate to rail against the immorality and corruption of Herod and his court. First, and most noteworthy, is John's denouncement of Herod's incestuous marriage to Herodias, who was the former wife of Philip, his brother (Matt. 14:3–4). As such, Herod's union with Herodias was prohibited by Leviticus 18:16.

But there is also a strong sense that John was condemning all of the general corruption Herod had brought to his office. We are told that Herod was "reproved" by John, not only for his sexual immorality but "on account of all the wicked things which Herod had done" (Luke 3:19). Herod's corrupt rule was part of a bigger problem of a nation that was not bearing the fruit of righteousness, and for whom judgment was impending (Luke 3:7–8). John's warning was stern and unmistakable: "And also the axe is already laid at the root of the trees; every tree therefore that does not bear good fruit is cut down and thrown into the fire" (Luke 3:9). First-century Israel was a tree, and God was giving notice through His prophet that He was about to cut it all down—roots, trunk, and branches.

When you review the writings of the founding fathers and our religious leaders during the American Revolution, it is remarkable how many times the metaphor of the nation of Israel is used. George Washington wrote of "the same wonder-working Deity, who long since delivering the Hebrews from their Egyptian Oppressors planted them in the promised land—whose providential agency has largely been conspicuous in establishing these United States as an independent nation."[4]

In her writings, Abigail Adams, the brilliant wife of John Adams, compared the defense of America to the rebuilding of the walls of Jerusalem under Nehemiah. Her husband, one of the prime catalysts for independence, wrote of his leadership position in America's early struggles for independence as akin to the struggles of Moses and the children of Israel.[5] Of course, it would be a major mistake to confuse Old Testament Israel with America, or any other nation, as a matter of precise theology. But it is clear beyond question that many of those involved in founding America felt a powerful presence of divine empowerment and destiny for that project—and the only way they could describe it was to refer back to God's visible and ever-present dealings with Israel.

John the Baptist was a voice from the rugged wilderness declaring the coming kingdom of Christ, the King. He was also a prophetic voice stressing the absolute moral values required in true kingdom living. He not only spoke to the people, but he also took his message to those in positions of civil authority—both to the lowest civil servants as well as the highest chief of state.

America has been blessed beyond measure by God's grace and protection. Our founding was a miracle. Our ultimate triumph of survival over the last two centuries is due to nothing less than the guiding hand of the Lord. But like any other nation, our continued success is doomed if we forget either the need for repentance or the need for works that are fitting for righteousness. Like the ancient Judea of John's day, it can be said that the axe may yet be laid at the root of America's tree of prosperity and power. It may be that more prophetic voices are needed, like John's, to give that last and most critical warning to a nation whose legacy and future hang in the balance.

4 | Answering the "Just Evangelize" Position

Perhaps the most persuasive argument in favor of a wholesale evangelical retreat from engaging in the culture war (although it is a misleading one) comes from nothing less than the Great Commission itself. In Matthew 28:18–20 Jesus communicated His great command to His disciples:

> And Jesus came up and spoke to them, saying, "All authority has been given to Me in heaven and on earth. Go therefore and make disciples of all the nations, baptizing them in name of the Father and the Son and the Holy Spirit, teaching them to observe all that I commanded you; and lo, I am with you always, even to the end of the age."

Those arguing for evangelicals to rearrange our cultural and political priorities remind us that the basic mission of Christ's Church is to evangelize. Politics, we are told, doesn't work any permanent change in the human condition—whether it is a broad moral condition in the society at large, or the individual condition of one man or one woman's life. Only the new birth through Jesus Christ will revolutionize a life, and only when we have sufficiently revolutionized lives in Christ will any long-lasting change take place in our families or our nation.

This argument has appeal because all evangelicals would agree that politics does not change hearts or souls. But the argument is a false one because it forces us into a false choice. Those who advance this argument are really saying that Christians can either win souls and devote themselves to the task of evangelism, *or* they can engage the culture and do battle for truth in the public arena—but they cannot do both.

We would argue that Christians not only *can* do both, they *must* do both. In fact, we would go so far as to say—and this may sound radical and extreme—that we are not truly evangelizing our world unless we penetrate the cultural institutions around us *even more* than we have been doing in the last three decades.

Franklin Graham Speaks Out

Billy Graham is truly one of the great evangelists of the twentieth century. His son Franklin, who is increasingly visible as an evangelist in his own right, is a wonderful example of integrating gospel faith with gospel action.

Franklin started Samaritan's Purse, a worldwide relief agency that puts Christian love into action. As a guest on the March 3, 2000 broadcast of *Janet Parshall's America*, he spoke out about the need for American Christians to actively oppose persecution of Christians abroad:

Parshall Franklin, this is an amazing story. We know the aggression is unbelievable, but there was a bombing recently. First and foremost, tell us how Samaritan's Purse has been involved in Sudan in the past.

Graham   The last two and one-half years, Janet, we have
been in an area about two hundred miles north of
the Uganda border, in the heart of the southern
part of the Sudan. We have a hospital that serves
about a hundred thousand people. And it's been
known to the government that we're there. There's
no military target in that area—it's just a wide spot
in the road where we have put in a mission station,
this little hospital.

And the day before yesterday, about midday,
Russian-built bombers flown by the Islamic government of Khartoum flew overhead and dropped
twelve bombs onto our hospital. Fortunately, two
of the bombs did not explode. Two people were
killed. Dozens were wounded. Six are critically
wounded—we're not sure they're going to survive.

Parshall   Even if one just has a small interest in international affairs, one would think that aggression
would primarily be meted out against military
sources and military sites. Why in the world,
Franklin, would they go after a hospital?

Graham   They do not want Samaritan's Purse in their country. We're one of the few hospitals that's open for
the blacks in the south. We have to remember that
the Sudan is a huge country in Africa. The northern half of the country is Arab—it's Muslim. The
southern half is black, tribal, Christian Africans. A
few years ago the government of Sudan instituted
what they called Islamic law, requiring everyone in
the nation—Christians as well as the Muslims—to
come under Islamic law. The Christians said,

"We're not going to do it. We want to be free to worship God the way we see fit." And they rebelled. They're actually fighting for their survival. Two million of these Sudanese have been killed. Janet, what I don't understand is that last year we started a bombing campaign against Yugoslavia because two thousand Kosovars had been killed. These are white Europeans, and this is, all of a sudden, genocide, and America and its allies must intervene. Two million blacks, though, can get annihilated—and our president says nothing about it, and does nothing about it.

Parshall   Franklin, we have a few heroes here in Congress. One of them is Senator Sam Brownback of Kansas, who recently made a visit to Sudan. Another is Senator Bill Frist of Tennessee. These men believe there is something that this government can do. What is it, and do you agree with them?

Graham   I agree with them 100 percent. First of all, we can put in sanctions—just like we did against Milosevic, just like we have done with Saddam Hussein. We can come in with a blockade, and we can shut down that country very easily. You can eliminate their air power—eliminate their ability to fly— and give the people in the south a chance at freedom. I believe that if the United States government led the way and put in this blockade, the Sudanese government would fold very quickly. Because the government of the Sudan is not even popular among the Muslims. They don't want this harsh law. They want to be free. So I think this is an illegitimate government. They came to power by force. They practice slavery.

Parshall The president's approach, when it comes to our relationship in international affairs, has been to suspend moral judgment. Yet he said that there was a moral imperative, paradoxically, that we get involved in the situation in Bosnia and in Kosovo. There is a moral imperative here, and one cannot suspend moral judgment when it comes to the issue of slavery. Would it not, then, behoove every man and woman of God to pick up the phone and call their U.S. senator and say, "I want you to encourage sanctions against the government of Sudan"? Money doesn't talk; it shouts. And economic sanctions would be a way of sending a message.

Graham No question. I think you should write your representative in Washington, but also write the Clinton administration. Because this president will do absolutely nothing unless he feels that the people are wanting it, and that the polls are demanding action. I think we have to write him as well as our elected leaders in Congress, and demand that something be done to end slavery as we go into this new millennium.

Parshall In the meantime, Samaritan's Purse—as you have just said—is going to stay because you believe unequivocally that God has called you to serve in that area. What can we do for Samaritan's Purse now?

Graham Because the Sudan is a war zone, it is dangerous. I would appreciate the prayers of people—that God would protect us and keep us safe, and that we would be in the position to continue to help these poor people in the southern Sudan, these black Africans who need so much help. They need love, and they need someone to speak on their behalf.

Parshall   Franklin, can we help financially as well? That hospital has to be rebuilt.

Graham   Not only do we want to repair the hospital and the damages, but we want to open up more satellite clinics. Anyone who wants to, we'd love to have their help. [Address: Samaritan's Purse, Box 3000, Boone, NC 28607. Web site: <www.Samaritan.org>.]

THE PRACTICE OF TRUTH FOR THE CHRISTIAN

Even in his earlier writings, Francis Schaeffer argued that the mission of the Church in witnessing, winning disciples, and building churches was to be seen in a broad and real-life context, rather than a narrow, hyperspiritualized "otherworldly" perspective.

In 1968 he wrote that, as the Christian Church finished its course through the second half of the twentieth century, it needed to perfect the practice of the truth of God. This, he observed, required the loving confrontation of antithesis—we must proclaim and stand for God's truth—and in so doing confront "what is false in theology, in the church, and the surrounding culture."[1] None of us relishes confrontation. Yet if we live out the practice of truth in a culture built, more and more, on distortion, manipulation, and hedonism, we must enter into confrontation. We must practice love in that confrontation. But we must also practice truth.

Later, in 1970, Schaeffer became more direct about the role

of the Church in the public issues of American culture. He identified the two warring political and social groups. One group was the "New Left elite," driven by humanism and bent on turning America away from its roots of historic Christian truth in favor of a radical view of individual autonomy. These are the new liberals.

The other group was the "Establishment elite," represented currently by those economic and free-trade conservatives who would value profit and commerce over justice and morality.

Schaeffer's conclusion was that the evangelical church must practice the truth, regardless of the strange partnerships it may engender:

> At times you will seem to be saying exactly the same thing as the New Left elite or the Establishment elite. If there is social injustice, say there is social injustice. If we need order, say we need order. In these cases, and at these specific points, we would be co-belligerents. But do not align yourself as though you are in either of these camps: You are an ally of neither. The church of the Lord Jesus Christ is different from either—totally different.[2]

By the 1980s, Francis Schaeffer's warnings about the decline of American culture and the clear and present danger to the Church became bolder. By that time the Supreme Court had wrested control of the abortion issue from all fifty states and declared, by constitutional fiat, that the right to destroy the unborn was a fundamental right. Moreover, the attacks against church autonomy and the stripping bare of traditional notions of religious liberty in the courts had crystallized the need for Christian action. His words had the shrill emphasis of the desert prophet trying to rouse the sleeping church: "Can we be so deaf as not to hear all the warning bells?" he cried out.[3]

In the almost two decades since Schaeffer's *Christian Manifesto*, it is doubtful that the majority of evangelical Christians have heard the warning bells—we have failed to engage the battle where it should be waged: namely, *everywhere.*

Yet this does not mean that we relinquish our commitment to gospel evangelism in favor of a spiritually empty social gospel. The twentieth century has already seen the fire of Holy Spirit revival replaced, in many of our churches, with social programs and Christian welfare bureaus.

Instead, we are called to integrate our witness for Christ to the world with the practice of the whole truth in the midst of a decayed culture.

A NEW TESTAMENT VIEW OF EVANGELISM

Most of us think of evangelism as, at its core, something along the lines of the pamphlet called the "Four Spiritual Laws," which Campus Crusade for Christ uses. Those four basic principles are:

1. God created men and women, loves them, and desires a personal relationship of fellowship with them.
2. Men and women have sinned and cut themselves off from fellowship with God.
3. God sent His Son, Jesus Christ, to make the perfect sacrifice for our sins and thus satisfy the requirements of a holy God.
4. We must individually appropriate and receive the benefits of this saving work of Christ by a personal faith in Jesus Christ as Savior and Lord.

While we can agree that this is the *core* of the gospel message, it cannot be the *entirety* of the gospel message. Like the ripples of a stone creating ever widening concentric circles, the truth we proclaim and demonstrate must start with this core in mind; but it will involve multiple rings of scriptural truth as revealed in the Bible.

Jesus did not begin His ministry by dumping a complex, generalized encyclopedia of theology on the heads of His disciples. During the course of His ministry, He progressively showed, through miracles, acts of compassion, parables, and didactic teachings, who He was and how we are to respond to Him.

For instance, Jesus knew that His miracle-working power, manifested in telling a lame man to walk, would authenticate the fact that He was the Son of God. Yet He explained that the greater miracle was really His ability to forgive sins and to heal the soul of the sinner who came to Him by faith. The fact is that Jesus did both. The lesser physical miracle authenticated and demonstrated the greater spiritual truth of His divine nature, and His power of perfect forgiveness. His "good deeds" in the mundane things of the physical world underscored his divine goodness. He practiced the truth of who He was in everything He did.

This does not diminish the fact that Jesus had pity on those who suffered or who were wronged. His motivation, as Scripture tells us, was out of the divine heart that felt compassion for the aching hearts and bodies of those around Him. But it does mean that while He was telling parables about the smaller particulars of what life in His Kingdom is like, He was also giving witness to the greater and broader principle—that He is King and that we can, by faith, become part of His kingdom family. In other words, the Lord Jesus not only proclaimed the coming kingdom of God, but He also demonstrated it in the miracles and acts of compassion that He performed.

When the apostle Paul was illegally arrested, in violation of his rights as a Roman citizen, we see in Acts 16:16–40 how he treated the cause of his arrest as an opportunity to practice truth in the same way. Paul had dared to disrupt the corrupt system of some spiritual counterfeits in Philippi. A fortune-teller had been following his missionary trail and using Paul's popularity to siphon off gullible new clients. When Paul exposed this pseudoreligious racket, it had an immediate negative impact on the profits of these local entrepreneurs (v. 19). The angered merchants conspired against Paul and had him arrested illegally.

First we see that Paul used his imprisonment to spread the good news of Jesus Christ (vv. 25–32). Here was classic evangelism. Yet when the time came to release him from his illegal confinement, Paul protested and refused to leave the jail. He forced the jailers to bring the magistrates down to the jail so they would be exposed to the truth of his unjust imprisonment (vv. 37–40). The great and broad truth of the gospel was vindicated and demonstrated in the particulars of his protest over the injustice of his illegal jailing. Paul stood firm for truth: whether it was the broad and universal truth of salvation through Jesus Christ, or whether it was the particularized truth behind official corruption and mistreatment at the hands of Roman officials.

Both of us know Christians who have been winsomely outspoken about Christ in their places of work and within their sphere of influence. Then some act of official corruption or injustice or evil took place. They had a choice to limit their concept of evangelism to the pure gospel of the Four Spiritual Laws, and thereby avoid becoming involved in the tough stuff of exposing evil and standing for truth. But if they had remained quiet, if they had looked the other way, what kind of message would they be sending? The message would have been that this

Jesus they preached is fine for the *spiritual* aspects of life, but that He really has no connection to the realities of life in the trenches, where it is muddy, cold, and dangerous.

Nothing could be more distorted than that kind of message. When our fellow Christians take a stand for the whole truth of the whole gospel, they illustrate the reality of Jesus Christ. When other believers in Jesus tell us that Christians should redirect their energies toward evangelism, and withdraw from the public square, we must remind them—lovingly, but firmly—that we can do the work of evangelism in every square inch of American life, as long as we consistently share the elements of the gospel message, and as long as we live lives that illustrate His truth. In doing that, we are penetrating the synagogue as well as the marketplace—the palaces of government as well as the tiny shacks of the downtrodden. And in living the message of Jesus in all of those places, we follow in His perfect footsteps.

5 | "Politics Is a Dirty Business" and Other Common Myths

OVER THE YEARS we have often heard the same objections to Christians actively engaging the culture. Yet each of these objections is built on a faulty premise. Here are some of the most common ones.

WHY SHOULD CHRISTIANS GET INVOLVED IN SUCH A DIRTY BUSINESS AS POLITICS?

We first started hearing concerns about the "dirty business" of politics many years ago. After addressing some issue dealing with education or abortion or some pending legislation we felt had posed an attack on families, we would open the discussion to questions from the floor. Inevitably, some well-meaning person would ask how Christians, who are called to be holy, could possibly be involved in such a low-down, dirty business as politics.

One of the most concise—and effective—responses to this argument comes from Pastor Tony Evans, a powerful Bible teacher who doesn't mince words or compromise the Word of God. Tony points out that rather than run from politics, Christians ought to ask God whether this is the exact place to which they are being called to minister. He wrote:

> There are believers out there who should be running for office. Politics is only as dirty as the people involved. The way to clean up politics is to put righteous people in office.
>
> This society needs people who feel God's call on their lives to serve him in politics. Then, we will have leaders like the ones Jethro told Moses to choose: "able men who fear God, men of truth, those who hate dishonest gain." (Ex. 18:21)[1]

There is yet a second problem with this argument about "clean" Christians and "dirty" politics. And that occurs when we take this argument to its logical extension. This point came up when the two of us hosted a radio roundtable discussion on *Janet Parshall's America* with Cal Thomas and Pastor Ed Dobson. Craig cited the page and paragraph from their book where they stated unequivocally that "politics and faith are irreconcilable. The former cannot tolerate zealotry, and the latter cannot tolerate compromise."[2] That statement implies that political compromise is part of that dirty business of backroom deals and smoke-filled rooms that Christians need to shun. But such a conclusion ignores the reality of our political process.

All kinds of compromises are made, and ought to be made, to get legislation out of committee, onto the floor, and voted on successfully. Not every compromise constitutes a compromise of moral dimensions. A decision to appropriate 1.2 million dollars rather than 1.5 million dollars to a budgeted item in a fiscal year may be the result of hard bargaining between members of an appropriations committee in Congress. However, that does not mean that the compromise was immoral or unsavory, any more than you are being immoral or unsavory the next time you engage in some hard bargaining at your neighborhood automobile dealership.

But even beyond that, as Craig pointed out in our radio discussion, we would end up achieving only folly if we consistently took the "dirty business" argument and applied it to all other fields of endeavor—or *any* other field of endeavor. How about professional sports? The evidence is that some (and certainly too many) professional sports figures engage in conduct off the field that would offend most of us, including drug use, violating the law, and sexually assaulting women, to name just a few unfortunate examples from the news. Talk about a dirty business! Does that mean that all Christians must get out of professional sports?

After sweeping the Christians out of sports, we can turn to business and industry. After all, history is full of stories of the robber barons of commerce. Moreover, the failures of the savings and loan industry of a few years back, due in some cases to the greed and fraud of the captains of finance, would likewise compel us to get all Christians out of the business world. If we follow this logic, we will end up withdrawing from every avenue of culture and retreating to the monastic life of desert hermits. Yet Christ never called us to retreat or to become totally insular. His Great Commission, "Go therefore and make disciples of all the nations," presupposes our penetration *into* the world—not a retreat *out* of it.

SHOULD CHRISTIANS FORCE THEIR MORALITY ON OTHERS?

The problem with the myth of Christians forcing their morality on others is that it makes a fatal assumption. It assumes that it is possible to legislate society without imposing one form of morality or another. Because Christians seek to "impose" a Judeo-Christian value system on our public policy, the argument goes, the rest of society has the right to cry "foul."

This assumption is an invalid one. The fact remains that it is impossible to regulate, legislate, or enforce codes of conduct in society without imposing some form of morality.

Norman Geisler, a noted evangelical thinker and theologian, and his coauthor Frank Turek make this point, using the debate over abortion as an illustration:

> Everyone realizes that "pro-life" people want to impose: They want to protect the baby and thus impose on the mother the duty of carrying her child to term. But what is so often missed in this debate is that "pro-choice" activists want to impose their morals on others, as well: They want to impose the morals of the mother on the baby and, in some cases, on the father. When abortion is the choice, the morals imposed on the baby come in the form of a knife, a vacuum, or scalding chemicals. Such a choice also imposes on the biological father by depriving him of fatherhood and the right to protect the child.[3]

The pro-choice segment of America is exalting a specific moral position. They contend that the *freedom* of women to make the choice for or against abortion, without interference from government or society, is the highest moral value. Freedom of choice is the moral value devoutly, consistently, and vehemently urged on our legal system by the pro-abortion forces. They are *imposing* that value system through the judicial, executive, and legislative branches of our government.

In contrast, Christian pro-lifers also agree that, *in general,* freedom of choice is a valid moral value; nevertheless, in the abortion context it is surpassed by a *greater* moral value—the sanctity of innocent human life.

The question, then, is not *whether* someone's moral values

will be imposed. Rather, the question is *whose* moral values we will permit our government to impose. As long as the effort of evangelical Christians to influence public policy does not run afoul of the Constitution or otherwise conflict with the moral and spiritual principles of the Bible, their efforts to impose moral values are as permissible (and certainly more preferable) than those of the skeptic, the atheist, or the secularist.

If Bible Prophecy Reveals God's Plan for the Nations, Why Fight It?

Another common objection to Christians engaging the culture especially in the arena of public policy, is the myth that the inevitability of God's prophetic plan for the nations renders our participation unnecessary. If God's prophets had followed this line of thinking, few of our Old Testament prophetic books would have been written. Most of the prophets were rejected and despised, and their message was held in contempt. Why did they persist in giving forth a harsh and unyielding warning when they knew that the children of the Lord would reject it? Was this not an exercise in total futility?

The prophets delivered their difficult messages to a hostile culture because they were obedient to God's call on their lives. They were faithful in the specific duty given to them by the Lord, and then trusted that He would use that duty in His inscrutable and perfect will. In other words, they trusted the results of their obedience to God alone.

The fact that we know the inevitability of God's broad plan for the planet does not give us the right to flinch from living out the truth of the gospel in our particular corner of the world. *What* God will do in the future winding-up of the history of the world has been settled in the pages of Scripture. However, *how and when*

He will do it is not as clear. One thing *is* clear, however. He has chosen, for reasons that are imponderable, to work His will through the Church, which is the repository of His Holy Spirit in the world. The theologian Lewis Sperry Chafer put it this way: "The most basic and fundamental reality respecting the Church is that she is a temple for the habitation of God through the Spirit."[4]

If the Church is doing what it should, then we will be doing God's work until He calls us out of the world. If we are His habitation, then we have the high privilege of being used by Him until He comes. We do not know exactly *how* we will be used to coordinate the details of His ultimate plan. The essence of faith, however, is the knowledge that we *will* be used.

A great example of this is the nation of Israel. Christians sometimes express considerable confusion about a proper Christian response to America's policy regarding Israel. Clearly, the Bible outlines the future of Israel in God's prophetic plan. But that does not mean that we should not actively support that nation when its integrity and survival are being threatened.

When Benjamin Netanyahu was prime minister of Israel, he was honored in Washington by a coalition of Christian ministries and Jewish organizations. Janet had the privilege of acting as the mistress of ceremonies for the event. This Judeo-Christian coalition came together in order to encourage Israel to maintain an undivided Jerusalem, and to urge it not to yield to pressures from the Clinton administration to give away its land-based security in return for questionable promises of future peace. Was this a political gathering? Quite the contrary. Although Mr. Netanyahu was a political leader, the meeting had a distinctly biblical mandate: to protect God's chosen people in God's chosen land and to "pray for the peace of Jerusalem."

When we were in Jerusalem recently, we had a great conversation with a local Jewish merchant. His shop was situated along the winding, narrow stone alleyway that leads into the Jewish Quarter of the city's homes and stores. He was a very skilled and successful artist—a tall, handsome man with a booming voice and a very obvious love for Israel, his homeland. As we talked on and as evening closed in, he began sharing with us how he had already served in three separate wars in Israel (and he was not much older than we are). We could hear the fatigue in his voice and see the weariness in his eyes. Israel, this small and beleaguered nation, is tired of constantly fighting for its survival. Its people need our prayers and our support. There is no greater calling for Christians who want to be salt and light than to work for the security and autonomy of the nation of Israel. America can either be a friend for Israel, or a foe. The former is a necessity; the latter would be a disaster. Though we know from the Bible that God is planning to consummate all of human history within the borders of that land in the future, Christians cannot be passive about Israel in the present.

When Christians come together with a common desire to act as God's hands and feet, and they do so in His Spirit and according to His Word, they are doing a great work—because it is His work. It is work that knows no geographical limits or international boundaries. After all, we work for a King who uses the planets as a footstool! That is why we can truly sing:

> That Thy way may be known on the earth,
> Thy salvation among all nations.
> Let the peoples praise Thee, O God;
> Let all the peoples praise Thee.
> Let the nations be glad and sing for joy;
> For Thou wilt judge the peoples with uprightness,
> And guide the nations on the earth. (Ps. 67:2–4)

6 | Reconstructionism and the Limits of Christian Action

A WHILE BACK Janet was on a television broadcast with one of the founders of the modern feminist movement. The subject was one where there had been a vigorous disagreement between Janet and her feminist opponent regarding the religious right. When the show ended and the cameras were off, the two of them walked to the elevator together.

Then this well-known feminist made a remark that was startling and might even strike some of us as bizarre. Her voice was urgent, and her look was that of a person who really believed what she was saying. She told Janet she had learned that a handful of Christian activists were working at that very moment to introduce legislation permitting the death penalty for certain sexual offenses, such as adultery. She said this explained the source of her fear of Christian conservatives.

Needless to say, the two of us know that Congress has no plans to stone homosexuals or adulterers. Those who keep a finger on the pulse of national and state legislation might be tempted to scoff at this feminist leader's suggestion. On the other hand, we have a pretty good idea where her information came from. It raises an issue that should be evaluated—and rejected—as the Church enters the new millennium. The source of this kind of idea comes from the concept of theonomy, also known as Christian reconstructionism.

THEONOMY: THY KINGDOM HAS COME

Theonomy is not exactly a word you use every day. From its Greek derivation it means the *law of God.* The term was coined by members of a Christian movement that believes in a reconstructionist view of culture. Three components of that position are essential. First, reconstructionists (or followers of dominion theology, as they are also known) accept the proposition that the laws and regulations of the Old Testament can be, indeed must be, translated into contemporary society. This view believes that the law of God (theonomy) as outlined in the Old Testament and in all of its details, is fully and perfectly applicable to our lawmaking function today.

Second, there is at least a presumed understanding that there is no real distinction between Israel (and God's dealings with it from Genesis to Malachi) and the New Testament church—or for that matter between Israel and America in the twentieth or twenty-first centuries. Those who advocate the reconstructionist position tend to reject the dispensationalist interpretation of Scripture. Dispensationalist theology believes God has used different strategies as He has dealt with the human race at different times in history (while nevertheless maintaining a perfectly consistent moral and spiritual master plan).

Charles Ryrie of Dallas Theological Seminary noted that this understanding of the Bible distinguishes "God's program for Israel from his program for the church. Thus the church did not begin in the Old Testament but on the day of Pentecost, and the church is not presently fulfilling promises made to Israel in the Old Testament that have not yet been fulfilled."[1] This rejection by reconstructionists, of the difference between Israel and the present church is central to understanding the problems with their view of culture and politics. One need not be a full-fledged dispensationalist to see the problems caused by equating all of God's dealings in the Old Testament with His dealings with humanity after the advent of the Church of Jesus Christ.

The third critical component of this form of dominion theology is the view that God's kingdom has either already arrived and it is up to Christians to bring it to full realization, or that we can, and will, bring about the appearance of His kingdom through "cultural Christianization."

Political commentator Garry Wills was astute enough to note the influence of dominion theology in the political scene of the late 1980s. While we could argue about whether Wills paints with too broad a brush in labeling some people as part of the reconstructionist movement, there is no question he understood the gist of that faction:

> "Dominion theologians," as they are called, lay great emphasis on Genesis 1:26–27, where God tells Adam to assume dominion over the animate and inanimate world. When man fell, his control over creation was forfeited; but the saved, who are restored by baptism, can claim again the rights given to Adam. Thus the true inheritors and custodians of this world are Christians who can "name it and claim it" by divine right . . . They resume authority under a revived covenant, renewing "Old Testament" law for modern times.[2]

THEOLOGICAL ERROR

The Old Testament law simply cannot be translated whole cloth into the present age. The mandate for the Christian today is different from the moral imperative placed on Israel in the Old Testament. This is not because God has changed since then. Rather, it is due in part to the fact that His revelation of truth throughout history, as set out in Scripture, has been progressive. The culmination of His revelation about Himself and His plan of salvation for all who would respond is found ultimately in His Son, Jesus Christ, as recorded in the New Testament. However, that revelation began in the Old Testament.

As we are told in Hebrews 1:1–3:

> God, after He spoke long ago to the fathers in the prophets in many portions and in many ways, in these last days has spoken to us in His Son, whom He appointed heir of all things, through whom also He made the world. And He is the radiance of His glory and the exact representation of His nature, and upholds all things by the word of His power.

Jesus is described as being foreshadowed by Moses, but as being substantially different from (and superior to) Moses as the builder of the house of God (Heb. 3: 1–6).

Christ is noted to be similar to (but because He is perfect, He is substantially superior to) the Old Testament high priests who mediated the sacrifices between God's people and God (Heb. 5:1–10; chaps. 7–9).

Further, many regulations of the Old Testament were ceremonial, in that they were for the purpose of foreshadowing the nature and the coming of Jesus, the Messiah:

> For the Law, since it has only a shadow of the good
> things to come and not the very form of things, can never
> by the same sacrifices year by year, which they offer con-
> tinually, make perfect those who draw near. (Heb. 10:1)

With the coming of Christ, the believer now lives out his relationship with the living God by faith (Heb. 11), which has implications for how the believer is to live in the present, while still looking forward with hope to the future (Heb. 12–13). But the coming kingdom of God is distinctly different from the present kingdoms of man. "For here we do not have a lasting city, but we are seeking the city which is to come" (Heb. 13:14).

There is a sense in which reconstructionists are right that the moral laws of the Old Testament can be a guide to our present public policy. Certainly laws against murder, theft, and perjury find their genesis in the moral code of the Bible and must be continued. Yet it is also clear that the New Testament does not treat all of the Old Testament moral codes as a perfect match with the obligations of Christians in this, the Church age.

For instance, as Christian commentators Thomas Ice and H. Wayne House point out, Jesus rejected the application of the Old Testament sanction of death by stoning for the adulteress; and Paul rejected the application of the old covenant Jewish law that would have required the man living with his father's wife to be executed, or that heretics to be put to death.[3]

Additional evidence that Jesus did not consider the Old Testament law on an equal parity with the Church is contained in the Sermon on the Mount. As the perfect teacher, He began with the ideals of kingdom living that would typify His followers (Matt. 5:1–16). These are popularly referred to as the Beatitudes.

Then He moved to the relationship between His teaching

and the Old Testament law. Jesus stated plainly that His mission was not to "abolish" the law but to "fulfill" it (Matt. 5:17). The requirements of the law were to be "accomplished" in the future (5:18). But His purpose was not to simply encourage a rigorous adherence to a moral code. Instead, those who were to "enter the kingdom of heaven" must first obtain a "righteousness [that] surpasses that of the scribes and Pharisees" (5:20). The experts in the Jewish law of that day spent their time trying to adhere to a complex set of rules of conduct. Jesus came in order to provide for us, through His sacrifice on the cross, the superior righteousness that is our only entrée into the kingdom of heaven. By substituting Himself on the cross for each of us, He has obtained a divine pardon for our crimes against heaven and has gifted to us, through our faith in Him, that new and perfect imputed righteousness necessary to bring us into the presence of a holy God.

This point is further amplified through the ministry of the apostle Paul. He was a "Jew's Jew." He was a Pharisee and a powerful member of the sect's ruling structure. Paul noted, "I was advancing in Judaism beyond many of my contemporaries among my countrymen, being more extremely zealous for my ancestral traditions" (Gal. 1:14). His credentials as a student and follower of the law were impeccable (Acts 22:3). Those credentials permitted Paul to address with great authority the intrinsic difference between the function of the Old Testament law under the prophets and the new covenant through faith in Christ (Gal. 3–4).

While Jesus and Paul at times took a view that *diminished* the punishments and sanctions that Old Testament law would have required, in other ways they urged that the mere letter of the law should actually be *exceeded* by a new kind of moral and spiritual attitude. When Jesus moved into the remainder of the Sermon on the Mount, He contrasted five examples where the Old

Testament treated certain types of conduct, but where He was commanding something *even more*. Five times Jesus referred to the teachings of the Law ("you have heard . . .") and then contrasted it with the higher ethic of the new kingdom attitude of the Church ("but I say to you . . .") (Matt. 5:21–48).

Paul emphasized that Christians are no longer under the law; nevertheless, we should not use our new spiritual liberty as an excuse to commit sin, but rather as a motivation to serve others through the love of God (Gal. 5:1–14).

Thus, the reconstructionist view of the Old Testament law as something that can be transposed directly into civil law in the Church age is fundamentally flawed.

HISTORICAL AND LEGAL CONFUSION

Followers of dominion theology often refer to the fact that America began as a Christian nation. Our task, they would argue, is to restore our nation to its prior spiritual status. We have no quarrel that spreading the gospel will cause people to come to Christ, and that the more people who come to Christ in America, the better their lives will become, and the better we will be as a society. Neither do we contest the fact that the Pilgrims came to America out of a Christian sense of mission. Nor do we disagree that there was a general Christian consensus among the early settlers and founders of this nation, and that we have fallen far from their original example.

However, we must emphasize a subtle, but very important, distinction from the position of the reconstructionists. They envision a Christian America historically, one that can be restored today politically and culturally. Unfortunately, in addition to their theological errors, they also proceed on a mistaken view of legal history.

Often dominion theologians cite the 1892 Supreme Court case of *Church of the Holy Trinity v. United States* to support their argument about America being a "Christian nation."[4] However, the way in which they rely on that court decision is misplaced. In order to understand the error, we have to understand the background and context of that case.

In *Church of the Holy Trinity*, the U.S. Supreme Court interpreted a congressional statute that prohibited (with certain exceptions for actors, artists, lecturers, singers, and domestic servants) any contract to pay for the transportation of aliens into the United States in order to encourage them to "perform labor or services" here. The Church of the Holy Trinity was in New York. It had entered into a contract to hire E. Walpole Warren, an English pastor, to come to America and pastor the church. The government commenced suit against the church, claiming that its contract with the English rector had violated federal law.

The Supreme Court, in an opinion authored by Justice Brewer, decided the matter in favor of the church. The Court did back then what it still does today from time to time: it interpreted a federal law in a way that avoided a direct conflict with the Constitution.

First, the High Court noted that the term *labor and services* should be interpreted to mean manual labor, as opposed to professional services: "The common understanding of the terms labor and laborers does not include preaching and preachers."[5]

Next, the Court discerned that only by excluding Rev. Warren and the New York church from the reach of the Act would its ruling give life to the real intent of Congress. The Court determined that the real "evil" Congress sought to eradicate was the importation of cheap, foreign manual labor into America's industries.

Last, but certainly not least, the Court noted that to rule otherwise would be to permit an Act of Congress to violate a basic rule of religious liberty: "No purpose of action against religion can be imputed to any legislation, State or Nation, because this is a religious people."

The Court then proceeded to give a remarkable and powerful testimony of the influence of Christianity in the founding of America. Christopher Columbus's commission from Ferdinand and Isabella recounted that they invoked "God's assistance." Sir Walter Raleigh carried with him the authority to enact regulations in the new colonies as long as they did not conflict with the "true Christian faith." The first charter of Virginia set forth the obligation and privilege of "propagating the Christian Religion to such people as yet live in darkness." The charters of the various colonies each contained references to God or to Jesus Christ. The Declaration of Independence invoked a divine "Creator" as the source of all true rights and liberties. The Court further noted:

> Every constitution of every one of the forty-five states contains language which either directly or by clear implication recognizes a profound reverence for religion and an assumption that its influence in all human affairs is essential to the well being of the community.

Lastly, as the Supreme Court explained, Article I, section 7 of the Constitution exempts Sundays (the Christian Sabbath) from the calculation of the ten days the president has to veto a bill passed by Congress; and the First Amendment further underscores the importance of religion by protecting it from any law "prohibiting the free exercise thereof," or "respecting" its "establishment."

All of this was the Court's way of saying that America is a Christian nation. "In the face of all these, shall it be believed that a Congress of the United States intended to make it a misdemeanor for a church of this country to contract for the services of a Christian minister residing in another nation?"

The answer to this rhetorical question was an obvious no. It was unimaginable, as Justice Brewer put it, to think that Congress would have intended to make it illegal for "any Baptist church [to] make similar arrangements with Rev. [Charles] Spurgeon; or any Jewish synagogue with some eminent Rabbi."

Thus, the reference to America as a "Christian nation" was to show the obvious absurdity in the argument, advanced by the government lawyers, that Congress could have intended for a Christian church to be criminally prosecuted because it employed a foreign pastor. The Court was referring to the abundance of evidence that Christianity was the consensus religion during the founding of America as evidence that Congress could not have intended that kind of absurd legislative result.

The reconstructionists misconstrue the *Church of the Holy Trinity* case as some kind of judicial declaration that the United States was an official extension of Christendom, or that Christianity was our official state position. The Court certainly intended no such declaration, and the language of its opinion belies that position.

It is perfectly biblical, as well as prudent, to work toward the creation of a "Christian nation"—only if by that we mean a nation made up of citizens who have freely chosen the Lord as their God. We can preach the gospel, live it out in our lives, and work for the enactment of public policy that is consistent with broad biblical principles. We can urge laws that respect the sanctity of life, the value of the individual, personal responsibility, and reflect moral absolutes because we believe that the core of the gospel is consistent with those values. Between the revival that can come from the preached and practiced Word of God and the reformation of our civic life that can come through a moral worldview, there is the hope of a Christian consensus once again, but only in that sense.

But this is different from a return to our status as a Christian nation as preached by the reconstructionists. They view America as a receptacle of God's direct and theocratic rule, much like Israel of the Old Testament. As evangelicals we should, instead, see the Church as the receptacle of God's Spirit, administering within the church, and ministering to others in the midst of a fallen world.

The fact remains that while God gave an explicit, revealed, biblical context to His creation of the nation of Israel, America, even with its rich Christian heritage, has no such claim. To confuse the two is a dangerous mistake; it will confuse the saints and hurt the legitimate efforts to map out a Christian strategy for the future.

Activism Without Borders

A little more than a decade ago, the two of us became involved in a particularly difficult and prolonged work with a number of pro-life leaders and activists. We have been involved in the pro-life movement in one way or another since the 1970s. But by the mid to late 1980s, large numbers of Christians were increasingly engaged in opposing abortion by nonviolent "rescues" at the doors of abortion clinics. The idea was to literally save those babies who were destined for execution inside the abortion facility by preventing the pregnant mothers from getting to the doctors who would do the killing.

The two of us became engaged in assisting those in the pro-life movement within our own expertise—Craig by spending endless hours conducting the legal defense of those arrested, and

Janet by acting as media spokesperson for the groups. It was a hot, muggy summer and we had become absorbed in a particularly turbulent lawsuit brought by the government against huge numbers of pro-lifers. Most of us, in the midst of the explosion of hostile media coverage, crowded and confused court rooms, and massive police arrests, seemed to be equally interested in forging a biblically based, sensible plan of action. We wanted to stand for God and His truth, yet it was also apparent that to do so would require a reliance on His Spirit and an uncompromising adherence to His principles in a confusing landscape.

In a meeting one hot evening, we had one of those "epiphanies" (not to put too spiritual a spin on it) where something became very clear to both of us. One leader in particular was talking about pushing matters to an increasingly more extreme—but still nonviolent—level. It was very obvious, though, that there were no biblical boundaries at work in his agenda. We began asking questions about where the scriptural limits were. We suggested that there were principles of God that ought to restrain all of us. The answers we received confirmed what we had feared. Because of this person's reconstructionist-type vision of tearing down and rebuilding society, the New Testament covenant and ethics of Jesus Christ seemed to have been lost in the dust. As a result, we ended up separating from that individual.

The vast majority of the pro-life movement, we have found to our joy, is motivated by the love of Christ not only for the preborn baby, but for the mother and even for the abortionist. The movement is nonviolent to its core and is committed to a biblical response to the horrendous slaughter of human life that America has permitted.

Still, as we enter the new millennium, we must be wary of the traps that can hinder our effectiveness as ambassadors of an eternal kingdom. That kingdom has not yet come—and will not come through the efforts of man, woman, church or government—but will appear only when God deems that we have reached that "fullness of time" according to His divine timetable. Until then, we must avoid the pitfalls of the two extremes that are equally problematic. On one hand, we must avoid withdrawal from the culture in cloistered enclaves, regardless of the reason. "Go into all the world" (Mark 16:15) would seem to have no limitation. Further, Scripture indicts those who refuse to do good to others because of cultural prejudice or hypocrisy—exemplified by the parable of the Good Samaritan or the case of Peter's early reluctance to consider Gentiles as part of God's family. On the other hand, we must equally reject the belief that we can reconstruct a Christian America through legislation, mandate, or force, based on a misconception of God's plan for nations. In Jesus' trial before Pontius Pilate, the crowd demanded the release of Barabbas, the political zealot and insurrectionist, rather than Jesus. Even so, by A.D. 70 the zealots had failed in their opposition to Rome, and Jerusalem was burned to the ground.

When Janet accompanied that feminist leader to the elevator that day, she was able to end the conversation by reminding her debate opponent that faith in Christ has nothing to do with legislating death for adulterers—but it has everything to do with a gospel of love to those who are lost. The other woman looked stunned—as if she had just heard for the very first time that the good news of the gospel really was good news, after all. When the elevator doors close on those kind of conversations in the twenty-first century, the Church will have done its job if both prayer and action—personal evangelism and social policy—have been done in a way that shows the world the love of God.

7 A Declaration of Principles: How We Ought to Live in a Millennium That Knows Not "Ought"

EVERY GREAT CAUSE needs a set of first principles. Perhaps the spiritual charter for Christians wrestling with how to live out their faith in the next century ought to begin with the words of Jesus:

> You are the salt of the earth; but if the salt has become tasteless, how will it be made salty again? It is good for nothing anymore, except to be thrown out and trampled under foot by men. You are the light of the world. A city set on a hill cannot be hidden. Nor do men light a lamp, and put it under the peck-measure, but on the lampstand; and it gives light to all who are in the house. Let your light shine before men in such a way that they may see your good works, and glorify your Father who is in heaven. (Matt. 5:13–16)

These verses, which obviously deal with how we ought to live as disciples of the Lord Jesus in the present, appear right in the middle of Jesus' Sermon on the Mount, which dealt so clearly with the values of His future kingdom—something we are tempted to associate with the hereafter.

This ought to be a clue to the most critical element of a Christian cultural compact for the twenty-first century. We do not live in His future kingdom in a physical sense now. But we are called to live out His kingdom principles as if we were already there—even now, even while we are surrounded by the ruined walls of a fallen world.

As the perfect Son of God, Jesus mastered the duality of being both man and God—being perfectly obedient to the Spirit while He was living in the flesh. We have a similar duality as believers. Paul wrote that even though we possess bodies of flesh and a sinful nature, we can be governed by Christ's indwelling nature until the ultimate redemption of our bodies at His coming and through our promised resurrection (Rom. 8:1–23).

In a corporate sense, also, we live in a similar duality—as citizens in the present fallen world, though we also have a greater citizenship in heaven. Unlike waiting for a bus at a bus stop, however, we don't just bide our time until we can be taken to our ultimate destination. Rather, we make known the reality of His kingdom *now* through the way we live—and through the way we make our lives have an impact. Each principle that guides our manner of living, our choices and values, and the way we speak out on issues must reflect the reality of this duality. The lives we now live, we live *through* Christ, and *for* His kingdom, while *in* the world.

The following, then, are ten basic principles we suggest as a kind of manifesto for the believer who wants to be salt and light in the decayed and darkened culture of the twenty-first century.

1. Though we are not saved *by* good works, we are saved *for* good works.

In Ephesians 2 we are told clearly what the grounds of salvation are. "For by grace you have been saved though faith; and that not of yourselves, it is the gift of God; not as a result of works, that no one should boast" (vv. 8–9). Through faith in what Christ did on the cross for us, and because of God's matchless grace, we are saved. Nothing we do by ourselves merits or earns this. We accept God's forgiveness of our sin as a free gift.

However, in the next verse Paul said, "For we are his workmanship, created in Christ Jesus for good works, which God prepared beforehand, that we should walk in them (v. 10).

Thus, although we have not been saved *through* or *by* the power of our good works, nevertheless we have been saved *for the purpose* of good works. "Good works" is the end goal of our having been "created in Christ Jesus" (i.e., our coming to faith in Him). In fact, as Paul told us, "God prepared beforehand, that we should walk" in a lifestyle of good works. From the very foundations of the world, God planned for those of us who have freely accepted the gift of salvation through Christ to "walk" in a lifestyle that impacts those around us—for our lives to be characterized by being His visible workmanship.

2. The good works to which we are called are not separate from matters of culture, social action, or politics.

There is a presumption among some believers that because Jesus never commanded His disciples to engage in politics, it represents an indictment against Christians becoming actively engaged in the culture. This fallacy is a little like the one about Jesus not mentioning to His disciples that it was permissible to use telephones; therefore, telephones must be evil. The absence of statements by Christ on any given subject is a poor argument for or against anything. While politics certainly existed in first-century Jerusalem and telephones didn't, the real point is that we must measure our involvement in contemporary culture, whatever the issue, by the general principles and precepts of Scripture—in other words, by what the Bible *does* say, not what it doesn't.

The politics of Jesus' day were vastly different from our modern system of representative, republican democracy. The mass of Jews of Jesus' time had virtually no right to participate in the decisions of government. Rome ruled the region, and both Herod (the Jewish puppet king) and the Sanhedrin (the religious ruling body over matters of Jewish worship and practice) governed only by permission of the Roman Empire. The average Jewish citizen had only one choice—to obey or to suffer.

But even in that oppressive system, Jesus told His followers that they must determine the proper scope of obedience to the state in consideration of their higher duty of obedience to God. Nothing in Scripture forbids Christians from involvement in cultural struggles *per se*. Yet there are clear biblical commands for us to be actively involved in performing good works.

While most of us think of good works as the acts of kindness and good will we perform for other individuals, we are also commanded to do good works corporately, for the good of the community and the nation.

Titus 3:1 says, "Remind them to be subject to rulers, to authorities, to be obedient, to be ready for every good deed." Notice how Paul linked the concept of obedience to the governing authorities with the idea of being "ready for every good deed." A few verses later the idea of good works is again emphasized. We are told "that those who have believed God" should "be careful to engage in good deeds. These things are good and profitable for men" (3:8). The phrase *good deeds* in the original language also has the meaning of *entering honorable professions.*

Good works then, include not only the private and personal acts we perform toward others, but also the group efforts of the Church in influencing the political and cultural environment.

3. All Christians are called to involvement in culture, the difference being only in the manner and in the measure.

Christian apologist Ravi Zacharias was correct when he reminded us of the sociologists' definition of culture: Culture is simply the way in which humans try to provide a coherent set of answers to life's greatest questions.[1] When we go to the theater, or listen to music, or join a political party, or debate the issue of abortion with a coworker in the lunch room or read a popular novel, we are engaging in the culture. In differing degrees, each of these activities puts us in touch with the current culture of America.

Jesus has called us to be observers of the moral, spiritual, and cultural climate of the times. He said to the multitudes: "You hypocrites! You know how to analyze the appearance of the earth and the sky, but why do you not analyze this present time?" (Luke 12:56). If we are disciples of Christ, we must not be like the multitudes who could predict the weather because they watched the skies but were ignorant of the existence of evil in their own time and woefully ignorant of Jesus Christ as God's spiritual antidote.

If we are to be effective communicators and steadfast defenders of gospel truth in a culture that is frantically searching for answers in all the wrong places, we must be astute cultural observers.

On New Year's Eve, 1999, the two of us watched the celebration of the coming new century as it was televised from the steps of the Lincoln Memorial in Washington, D.C. One particularly telling moment came as huge outdoor JumboTron video screens aired the premiere of Steven Spielberg's short-subject film on the history of America. Through his immense cinematic talent and understanding of film as a vehicle for storytelling, Spielberg has become a cultural prophet for America. His movies are not only hugely popular entertainment but they also carry a definite view of the world. As cultural phenomena, Spielberg's films offer answers to questions that are interwoven in the threads and tapestry of everyday life. If Christians are asleep as we enter this new millennium, they will miss the critical signs of the times that films like his are giving us.

Spielberg's short-subject film, shown to hundreds of thousands who had gathered on the Mall and viewed by millions on television, was no exception. It was masterfully edited. The musical score by former Boston Pops conductor and composer John Williams was poignant.

The film's view of America was loosely divided into five components. The first dealt with our industrial progress and prosperity. The second portrayed our ability to achieve victory in times of war. American achievements in athletics, popular entertainment, and art came third. Then we saw America's struggle over social justice, centering primarily on past battles for racial equality. Lastly, Spielberg gave us the ultimate secular vision of hope for the future: the power of science and technology coupled with man's ingenuity and willingness to explore the unknown.

Noticeably absent was any acknowledgment of the majestic and providential hand of God in the history of our nation. This was particularly surprising, given the setting of the event: right in the epicenter of Washington's marble monuments—each of them, in their own way, bearing a carved reference to the name of God. Yet there was no reference to the importance of religious freedom in the film, nor of the overwhelming reality that at any given time in American history some 80 to 90 percent of all Americans not only believe in God but also believe that He intervenes in human affairs. When Patrick Henry rose in the Virginia statehouse to rally Virginians to vote for independence from England in 1775, he appealed to the truism that "we fight not our battles alone. There is a just God who presides over the destinies of nations." A voice like Patrick Henry's has no place in much of Hollywood's cultural wisdom today.

Spielberg and the great mass of other popular artisans have erased the God of history from the cultural landscape of America and tried to replace Him with the promise of human ingenuity. We have witnessed the dawn of a new century. But the bright banners we see flying against the rising sun are those of secularists and humanists, not the faithful pilgrims of the *Mayflower*.

As a result, there is literally no place in America where the Christian is not desperately needed to stand fast, to speak out, and to live righteously. Never before has there been a greater need to speak and live the whole truth of the whole gospel.

4. All cultural, social, and political issues require a Christian response grounded in Scripture.

Think about the example of Jesus Christ. Was there ever a time when He decided that a question put to Him did not deserve an answer?

When Jesus was dragged before the high priest in an illegal fashion and questioned, He initially kept His silence (Matt. 26:59–63). His silence was in fulfillment of Isaiah 53:7, as well as in reliance on the Jewish law that recognized the equivalent of our Fifth Amendment right to silence. For crimes warranting death that law required proof *only* upon the strength of testimony of two or more witnesses, and not through a forced confession of the accused. But when the high priest pressed into Him with the ultimate question, "whether you are the Christ, the Son of God," Jesus broke His silence and laid the truth out plainly, clearly, and powerfully (Matt. 26:63–64).

Occasionally Jesus responded to a question with another question. Sometimes He answered not the question that came from the other person's mouth but the question in that person's heart. But Jesus gave a response to every question.

There is no serious question or issue in our troubled culture that does not deserve a Christian response. This does not mean quoting Scripture at every school board meeting or town hall gathering. But it does mean presenting a reasoned opinion consistent with the principles and precepts of God's Word.

Some people suggest, however, that many issues really have nothing to do with our stance as believers in Christ. We have often heard it said, somewhat sarcastically, that there is no distinctly Christian response on the issue of congressional term limits, for example. That issue engenders a difference of opinion among Christian conservatives whom we admire in both camps. Yet that does not mean there is no Christian response. What it means is that there is more than one good Christian response to the issue; it is up to us to decide which is the best. (The need to distinguish those issues that are reasonably debatable, from a biblical position, from those that are not is addressed in principle five below.)

Yet even in the mundane matters of a balanced budget, the Federal Reserve, commercial regulation, or foreign policy, we are called back to a basic understanding of the role of government in a God-created universe. Consider, for a moment, just a handful of principles from the Bible that bear on the role of government and culture in the life of the believer, and how these principles can guide us in a variety of public issues.

The Bible shows that the dual purposes of government are to restrain evil and to promote good (Rom. 13:3–4). It also says that we have obligations to both Caesar and God (Mark 12:17); yet when the two come into conflict, our primary obedience must be to the Lord (Acts 5:29). Scripture also tells us that the surrounding evil of our culture can oppress even the righteous, as Lot was oppressed by the wickedness of his community in Sodom and Gomorrah (2 Peter 2:7). Because God creates life and sanctifies it (Ps. 139:13–16), we should protect innocent lives from immoral destruction (Ex. 1:16–17). God had established nations and national boundaries for His divine purposes (Acts 17:26–27); when man (or Satan) attempts to concentrate and centralize global power, it is inconsistent with God's economy (Gen. 11:1–9; Rev. 17:15–18). As for the issues of finances, the entire book of Proverbs contains principles of wise stewardship of resources, lending and borrowing practices, and asset conservation and investment.

Taking just these few ideas from Scripture, we see that there *can* be a truly Christian response to criminal justice, public works projects, religious and individual liberties, sexual immorality, abortion, national sovereignty, limited government, foreign policy, and the federal budget. In truth, the burden of proof is not on the *Christian* to prove that he or she should have a biblically sound reaction to the issues of the day. Rather, the burden of proof is on those who would somehow feel that some issue is *beyond* biblical analysis. We have yet to see such an issue.

Beginning with the starting point that Christians are commanded to respond to the cultural, social, and political issues of the day, the question next becomes *how* we are to respond. Here we are commanded to grow up in Christ by "speaking the truth in love" (Eph. 4:15). This means that we are to be grounded in truth. Truth, at its essential core, is noncompromising and unwavering. Thus, "we are no longer to be children, tossed here and there by waves, and carried about by every wind of doctrine" (Eph. 4:14).

We are also to speak not just truthfully, but also lovingly. Unlike the world, which practices the "trickery of men" and "craftiness in deceitful scheming" (Eph. 4:14), speaking the truth in love means that we do not manipulate language to disguise the truth. It also means that we do not communicate our position with a mission to destroy or to defame others. We communicate truth with the primary goal of restoring, building, and redeeming.

5. Discernment and the right application of biblical truth can separate those Christian responses that are reasonably debatable from those that are not.

One of the challenges we face in the new century is to distinguish the "debatable" from the "clearly settled" issues. When the central premise of any Christian position is constantly under attack, revision, and criticism from within the Church, we will never get to the point of mapping out and then implementing a strategy to change things. It is amazing how even now, more than twenty years after the evangelical church focused its attention on the abortion issue, how muddled the thinking of Christians can be on the concept of the sanctity of life. If we had adequately communicated the scriptural basis for the pro-life position in our churches, Bible studies, and para-church ministries in the beginning, we might have been able to ignite the moral imagination of Christians the way the slavery issue in England ignited the moral imagination of Christians there in the nineteenth century.

Today the two of us often hear evangelical Christians express utter confusion over the most basic questions about issues like euthanasia, abortion, fetal experimentation, homosexual rights, and surrogate parenting arrangements. To be sure, these ethical questions are complicated and worrisome. But the Bible provides a starting point to deal with all of them. Each of these social aberrations arose because of a willful disregard for God's principles. We need to read no farther than the first four chapters of Genesis to find the foundations for a biblical apologetic against each of these practices.

The Church needs to establish a line of demarcation. We need to identify those matters that are so firmly rooted in Scripture that they are beyond debate. Then for each of those issues we need to courageously forge an agenda for the twenty-first century and to challenge each believing Christian to play his or her part.

6. The success of our Christian witness and works must be measured by more than mere winning or losing.

We are called to preach, teach, and practice the truth of Christ in times that appear to be increasingly stressful. Yet while we must courageously practice the truth in arenas that may be hostile to our message, we have to be careful not to adopt the world's measurement of success.

It was once said of Senator Everett Dirksen of Illinois, the seasoned and iconoclastic former Speaker of the House of Representatives, that he had the practiced wisdom to know not only how to count the votes but also how to make his vote count. The practice of truth for the Church in the twenty-first century will require that we stand for more than merely being able to count the votes. We will be required to make our lives count for Christ. Sometimes that will mean that when we apply the practical and effective use of political or cultural influence, then positive, tangible results will be obtained. We hope and pray, of course, for those tangible success stories. But that will not always be the case.

God does not require, nor does He guarantee, success in the worldly sense when we stand fast for Him. His Word makes the *uncertainty* of the outward signs of such success a *virtual certainty*.

In Hebrews 11, the great chapter of faith, we see this with crystal clarity. In the first thirty-five verses we witness a great parade of heroes of the faith. We are encouraged in those verses by the long list of miraculous triumphs granted by God. Noah and his family were miraculously saved from the flood. Abraham was miraculously led into an unknown land to found the nation of Israel. The blessings of God upon Isaac, Jacob, Joseph, and Moses are reminders of His grace. Even Rahab, the lowly town harlot, had her exercise of faith and her deliverance by God memorialized forever in the words of Scripture.

Yet right in the middle of one verse, the scenery changes and the skies darken (v. 35). We are told that others who were just as faithful to the God of Abraham, Isaac, and Jacob were "tortured" and "others experienced mockings and scourgings, yes, also chains and imprisonment. They were stoned, they were sawn in two, they were tempted, they were put to death with the sword; they went about in sheepskins, in goatskins, being destitute, afflicted, ill-treated" (Heb. 11:35–37).

There is no different standard of success between those who escaped catastrophe and those who were called to endure it. If America, in the coming decades, should sink into obscurity, disintegration, or even something worse, the failure will not be ours as long as we have stood firm for the Lord of hosts and have been fearless to live out His truth.

Scripture does not indicate that any of the Old Testament prophets who courageously delivered God's message, but were scorned and rejected because of it, were failures merely because the hard and stony soil of their culture rejected their seed.

Because we worship a God who is both limitless and infinitely compassionate, we can work and pray toward revival in our land. When Jonah chose to be obedient, put aside his own interests, and preached the message of the Lord to the despicably pagan nation–state of Nineveh, one of the greatest spiritual revivals in all of history exploded. The entire kingdom, some one-half million souls, bowed in obedience to the Lord. Even the king repented in sackcloth and ashes. If Nineveh the great, the powerful, and the wicked could experience this kind of revival, then there is still hope for America.

7. The impact of our Christian witness and works requires an understanding of evil and a practice of righteousness.

Few places can evoke an immediate awareness of the power and the reality of evil. Those who have visited the preserved buildings and ovens of the concentration camp at Auschwitz have remarked to us that this is such a place.

For us, we often think back to a trip we took years ago to Mexico. We poked around the Mayan ruins in the jungles of the Yucatán Peninsula, amazed at this ancient civilization that was so advanced. The Mayans had an advanced understanding of mathematics and science and had even constructed a sophisticated astronomical observatory. Yet a hundred yards or so from their immense stone pyramids and palaces at Chichén Itzá is a place that, for us, seemed to be the incarnation of evil. It is called the Cenote (Sacred Well) of Sacrifice.

The Cenote is a natural well of huge proportions that created a gaping hole in the floor of the jungle. It was hundreds of feet across and plunged down into a deep, dark pool of water below. Archeologists have mined the depths of this great shaft. What they found there is ugly testimony to the fact that great cultural and scientific accomplishments of a society do not eradicate the reality of sin or moral depravity. At the bottom of the well, mired in the silt of the ages, lay the bones of children sacrificed to the pagan gods of the Mayans. The children were drugged, then wrapped with ropes and cloth, and weighted down with stones. Then they were tossed in the well. There is some conjecture whether the children had been killed and their hearts cut out (a common practice in Mayan sacrifice) before being thrown into the black abyss.

For most of us, the centuries have obscured the great achievements of Mayan literature, language, mathematics, and a calendar system so ingenious that it was more accurate than the Gregorian system we use today. What remains in Chichén Itzá—along with its empty temples to pagan gods and its decayed athletic courts—is its name, which means "in the mouth of the well." It must forever be remembered for its moral atrocities—a living testament to the awful existence of evil.

America is not Chichén Itzá. But we are coming close—perilously close. Christians must take seriously the difference between sin and righteousness, between light and darkness.

In the twenty-first century will we find the courage to

denounce the darkness and exhibit the light? Listen to what the apostle Paul said:

> Do not participate in the unfruitful deeds of darkness, but instead even expose them; for it is disgraceful even to speak of the things which are done by them in secret. But all things become visible when they are exposed by the light, for everything that becomes visible is light. For this reason it says,
>
>> "Awake, sleeper,
>> And arise from the dead,
>> And Christ will shine on you." (Eph. 5:11–14)

8. The idea of culture—including art, science, and politics—is not inherently evil.

The Church seems to have a running love-hate relationship with culture. Either we dive into it, absorbing its secular values and adopting its crude fads, or else we try to shun it altogether, in order to avoid being carnal and worldly. The proper approach, we believe, lies somewhere in the middle.

We must begin with the first principle that culture, *per se*, is not inherently evil. The defilement of sin comes not from the exercise of the senses, but from the human heart (Mark 7:18–23). It is the human heart that brings forth "evil thoughts, fornications, thefts, murders, adulteries" (Mark 7:21). Paul warns of the false asceticism of a theology that is primarily one of "Do not handle, do not taste, do not touch!" (Col. 2:21).

We have permitted art, music, theater, and film to be almost entirely controlled by those who not only fail to articulate a Judeo-Christian worldview but are even openly hostile to it. At the same time, we have constructed neither a viable environment of Christian culture able to compete with the secular marketplace, nor a unified vision of what Christian art and culture ought to look like. While there are always brilliant exceptions, they are few and far between.

It has been thirty years since Francis Schaeffer urged us to quit merely shaking our heads or laughing self-righteously at the expressions of ugliness in contemporary art and culture. He pleaded with us to take these creative forms seriously—and to provide answers in our Christian apologetic and our Christian art to the dark nothingness at the core of the modern vision of life.

When the first-century Christians huddled together in the catacombs, their lives in constant danger, they scratched the artistry of their faith onto stone walls. One early tombstone of a Christian bore a picture of a cross in the form of an anchor with two fish dangling from its hook—a creative pictorial of the Christian's call to be fishers of men. This is the essence of Christian culture—to use whatever tools are available, even in a hostile environment—indeed, even in persecution—to creatively communicate the truth.

Our good friend Ted Baehr did this when he founded the Christian Television and Film Commission. Ted gives Christian families a reliable guide to what is good and bad in cinema though his movie reviews. His organization also gives out awards to folks in the filmmaking industry who produce movies that are uplifting both spiritually and artistically. As a Christian presence in Hollywood, Ted is adding salt and light to an art form that has been predominated, at least recently, by an anti-Christian bias.

The Church cannot be contented to simply rage against the darkness. We cannot merely complain about the sewage of popular entertainment. What our culture needs is for Christians to rise up and create a powerful, skillful, and biblical alternative.

9. If Christians abandon their culture, then it will have no other choice but the values of hell.

Most Christians are not called into work that brings them into daily contact with the cutting edge of what is worst about America. We know some Christians, for example, who are involved in the kind of law enforcement that would give the rest of us nightmares. Tracking serial killers and child molesters is work that takes a special type of fortitude.

Surprisingly, some of our friends have reacted the same way to the work we have done in the cultural, legal, and political areas. Dealing with abortion supporters, tyrannical bureaucrats who attack families from a "children belong to the village" mentality, vicious advocates of the homosexual movement, and self-proclaimed haters of the religious right can leave one feeling discouraged about the future of our nation and Christians' place in it.

Every once in a while the light breaks through the fog, and we realize what is at stake. Recently a book called *Understanding Homosexuality, Changing Schools—A Text for Teachers, Counselors, and Administrators* floated into Janet's radio studio. The book, fresh off the presses of a Colorado publishing house, was written by Arthur Lipkin, a founder of the Gay and Lesbian School Issues Project at the Harvard Graduate School of Education. He is an educational expert who trains teachers to go out and teach the youth of our future.

The book is a carefully constructed agenda for school administrators and teachers to inculcate a pro-homosexual perspective in our public education system. It is a detailed, heavily researched, 367-page treatise on how to change schools so they will be more favorable to the gay and lesbian position. Lipkin's goal is to integrate "gay and lesbian topics into the core of learning," "to increase tolerance for sexuality differences" in school, and to "facilitate the integration of gay/lesbian families into the school community."[2]

What kind of values are the focus of this new tolerance? One example is instructive. The author lavishes praise on a federal court decision in Massachusetts. It was a case that had special meaning for us. When Craig was the East Coast regional coordinator for The Rutherford Institute, he had provided consulting assistance to the group of pro-family attorneys who represented the parents in that lawsuit. The facts were bizarre and almost otherworldly, considering the affront to the decency of families in that public school district.

A crude sexuality/AIDS program called "Hot, Safe, and Sexy" was presented without parental notification or consent. Middle school students were herded into the school auditorium to withstand ninety minutes of a sexuality program that was long on "hip" sex jokes, short on information, and void of values. Students were invited on stage to simulate a sexual experience in front of their peers, and a young girl was then encouraged to pull a condom over a young man's head, to gales of laughter in the auditorium. Students who tried to avoid attending were told they would be punished if they skipped the program. When the parents sued school officials on the ground that their fundamental parenting rights had been violated, the federal court held (among its many other unfortunate rulings) that the legal rights of parents are currently so ill-defined in the law, and the rights of schools so near-absolute, that the school district should not be held responsible for the insult caused to the families and their children.

For Professor Lipkin, however, the court decision represented a "major triumph." He called the school district officials responsible for this hour-and-a-half educational monstrosity "principled school people" whose views made them "progressives," while the complaining families were merely "disgruntled parents."[3]

Well, you may say, at least when this new wave of totalitarian tolerance for promiscuity and perversion sweeps into our neighborhood schools, Christian children will certainly be permitted to be exempt from these programs as long their parents voice an objection. This is where Christians must shed their naiveté. The two of us have rarely felt the wrath of the secularistic status quo as keenly as when we dared to speak up on behalf of conscientiously objecting parents. Some of the language in these mandatory educational AIDS/sexuality/homosexuality programs would make Blackbeard and his gang of pirates blush. However, judging from the reaction of school administrators, you would think that exempting Christian children from this type of instruction posed a threat to national security.

Where do the proponents of "tolerance" like Professor Lipkin stand on exempting children? According to him such an opt-out approach should only (if ever) be used "as a last resort." Lipkin warns of dire results if parents are allowed to remove their children from blatantly offensive homosexuality instruction: "School authorities should consider where [opt-out clauses in their school policies] might lead . . . would creationists excuse their children from biology classes? . . . What begins as parental rights could transform classrooms into shifting masses of ideological pawns."[4]

If you have children or grandchildren, and if you are like many Christians who find it hard to afford Christian education, then issues over educational choice and school vouchers, sex education, and accountability of school officials to parents will become a critical struggle. If the Church continues to abandon these moral turf battles, the values that will belong to our nation tomorrow will increasingly reflect the philosophies of hell rather than the eternal principles of heaven.

10. Though God's kingdom will come only by His hand, our effort is still needed to reflect the character of its heavenly king in the meantime.

Under our present system of government, those "things that are Caesar's" for which we have responsibility (Luke 20:25) include all of the aspects of our active participation as citizens. There are limits, however, to our interaction with the public sphere.

The limits on our rendering to Caesar are three-fold. First, our conduct must not conflict with our higher duty to God. This is clear from Jesus' statement that we must render to God those things that have been distinctly reserved by God.

Second, our conduct must be in conformity with the principles of Scripture; it must be Christ-honoring and led by His Spirit. One of the simplest, yet most difficult, of these precepts involves the supremacy of love in all we do. Paul reminded us that the performing of great works, the moving of mountains because of a great personal faith, the living a life of total sacrifice for those in need, and even the placing of a life on the altar of persecution for God all come to nothing if not motivated by the love of God. Otherwise, we become merely a "clanging cymbal" (1 Cor. 13:1) rather than a part of God's great symphony.

Third, we must be aware that our efforts, regardless of how noble and committed, cannot establish the kingdom of Christ on earth. Jesus pointed out the futility of that approach in His dialogue with Pilate: "My kingdom is not of this world. If My kingdom were of this world, then My servants would be fighting, that I might not be delivered up to the Jews; but as it is, My kingdom is not of this realm" (John 18:36).

The two of us recall visiting the Judean wilderness of Israel. It is a stark and foreboding area of desert. We saw the dusty, jutting hills, barren of any vegetation or water—the spot, according to tradition, where Jesus was tempted during His forty-day fast. We traveled there when the sun was setting, and even at night the hot winds were gusting around the jagged cliffs and through the narrow valleys of rock. During the day the wilting desert sun beats down mercilessly. We think of Satan's attempt, there in that barren landscape, to tempt the Son of God.

Jesus had been in the desert for more than a month without food, water, comfort, or companionship. One of the temptations from the Evil One was this: "Again, the devil took Him to a very high mountain, and showed Him all the kingdoms of the world, and their glory; and he said to Him, 'All these things will I give You, if You fall down and worship me'" (Matt. 4:8–9).

Power and glory are enticing commodities. In Washington, D.C. they are the coin of the realm. Satan was clearly using his best shots for the Son of God. The answer Jesus gave the devil is the same answer He gives us today when we are tempted to try to establish, through human means, God's kingdom on this tired planet, or when we are tempted to let power or glory motivate and capture us. "Then Jesus said to him, 'Begone, Satan! for it is written, YOU SHALL WORSHIP THE LORD YOUR GOD, AND SERVE HIM ONLY.'" (Matt. 4:10).

We serve God in the midst of the cities and kingdoms of man. But we do so with our hearts fixed on a higher place.

8 | The Christian Light in the Ancient Cities

WHEN JANET AND I debate groups like Americans United for Separation of Church and State, one of their favorite diatribes is to accuse conservative Christians of trying to establish a theocracy in America. For instance, their magazine has aired the view that some evangelical leaders supposedly want "America to become a fundamentalist Christian theocracy."[1] Such an argument would be comical if it were not so tragically effective (yet wholly inaccurate) in painting conservatives as extremists.

This "theocracy" mantra is designed to frighten Americans into believing that evangelical churches want to turn the United States into a Christian version of Iran. Theocracies are, by definition, forms of government which are entirely religious in form, in structure, and in the content of their laws. One form of religion is *imposed* upon everyone—and everyone in that society is *required* to obey that one form of religion.

In order for Christians to be able to answer these outlandish charges, we need a bit of a history lesson. The history of the relationship between church and state seems to be one of two dangerous extremes. At one end of the spectrum there were pagan societies that cruelly persecuted Christians without hesitation. At the other end of the spectrum there have been some attempts at imposing Christian religious obligations on the entire citizenry of a nation. When it comes to these two extremes, we need to know history in order to avoid repeating it.

CONSTANTINE: THE MAN WHO WOULD BE CONQUEROR AND "CHRISTIAN KING"

The history of the centuries following the birth of the Church is the history of warfare, conflict, and conquering armies. Until the time of Constantine, the Roman emperors were thoroughly pagan. They often persecuted and slaughtered Christians, viewing them as just one more rebellion to the established order of Rome.

But something quite amazing occurred at a place called the Mulvian Bridge, which spanned the Tiber River. Some of the great battles of the past—the kind that turn the direction of whole nations around—have taken place at bridges. The year was A.D. 313. Constantine, the son of a Roman ruler, was preparing to wage war for control of the Roman Empire. His opponent, Maxentius, who actually had the advantage with his superior numbers, had retreated with his army inside the walls of the city of Rome. However, Maxentius decided to leave the protection of the city and engage Constantine at the Mulvian Bridge.

Constantine was far from being a Christian. But unlike the typical Roman pagan, he believed in monotheism—the existence of a single God. Furthermore, like his father before him, he had opposed the ruthless persecution of Christians on general moral principle.

On the eve of this great battle, Constantine had a dream. In the dream he saw the letters of the name of Christ together with the words: By This Sign You Will Conquer (*Hoc Signo Vinces*) appearing in the sky with the sign of the Christian cross.

Constantine took this to be a powerful omen, and on waking the next morning he ordered his soldiers to paint the sign of the cross on their shields as a symbol of their trust in the God of the Christians. The armies of Constantine waded into battle and were victorious. The opposing general, Maxentius, ended up drowning in the river. When Constantine marched into Rome as the conquering hero, he did not perform the traditional rites of thanks to the Roman gods. Constantine's loyalties were fixed: he would be on the side of this Christ of the Christians, who had apparently given him such a clear victory.

It is not clear whether Constantine really believed the Christian faith, or whether he merely used it as a matter of clever politics and strategy. However, it is clear that he ended up being the first politician (and certainly not the last) to use Christianity as a political lever. Making Christianity the official arm of the state resulted, however, in the theological and ecclesiastical corruption of the church. Under Constantine, the relationship between church and state had created enormous problems. In the eastern part of the empire, the state totally dominated the church until the Christian church was sapped of its spiritual vitality. In the west, the church slowly began to dominate the state, turning the church into a political hierarchy. By this time the Roman Empire had weakened considerably, and it was nearing the eve of a fearsome invasion that would shake its very foundations.

One thing, though, is undisputed: Constantine was able to put an end to the terrible persecution of Christians as an official dictum of the existing government, and thus began an unprecedented era of accommodation to Christianity. The lesson for

Christians today is that we must act so as to help insure the protection and accommodation of the Church while not falling prey to the dangers of becoming absorbed into the established state order. The balance required in avoiding both extremes is one of the great tasks of the Church. How to accomplish that task was something contemplated by one of the most influential Christian thinkers of all time—Augustine.

AUGUSTINE: THE SEEKER WHO FOUND TWO CITIES

Augustine lived during the time just following the reforms of Constantine (A.D. 354–430). He was considered the greatest expositor of Christian theology since the apostle Paul. Yet, like Paul, Augustine seemed to be an unlikely candidate for that position. He was raised in the North African area of Numidia, in a city called Thagaste. His mother, Monica, was a devout Christian; but his father, Patricius, was a Roman pagan. Augustine lived during the twilight years of the Roman Empire. While Constantine had officially created a Christian state, much (if not most) of the population was probably not authentically Christian in their walk or their beliefs.

In the midst of this turbulent time of political and religious upheaval, Augustine appeared on the scene. He was a brilliant scholar, and his parents (who were apparently of some financial means) sent him to the best schools. He was hired as a professor of rhetoric in Carthage, a great commercial and political center on the Bay of Tunis. Augustine was a seeker and had a brilliant mind. He became well versed in the prevailing philosophy of Plato, but he was forever seeking and searching for an ultimate anchor for his restless soul.

Augustine was also a hedonist who would have found solace in the playboy philosophy of Hugh Hefner in the twentieth century. Although he followed the traditions of the time and permitted his parents to betroth him to a future bride, he was far from a faithful bridegroom-to-be. At the time of his betrothal, he had been carrying on a long-term sexual affair with another woman, who bore him a son. He later had a sexual relationship with yet another woman.

Meanwhile, his philosophical and spiritual quest for wisdom intensified. Augustine joined a group of friends who had committed themselves to reading, meditating, and pursuing the ideal life of philosophical truth. Augustine was increasingly miserable, however. He yearned, in his scholar's mind, for a life of holiness that would be in tune with a higher and more transcendent truth. In his body, though, he compulsively sought worldly pleasures that only degraded him. This conflict created a breaking point. Augustine was a perfect picture of the apostle Paul, who cried out:

> For I know that nothing good dwells in me, that is, in my flesh; for the wishing is present in me, but the doing of the good is not. For the good that I wish, I do not do; but I practice the very evil that I do not wish . . . Wretched man that I am! Who will set me free from the body of this death? (Rom. 7:18–19, 24)

One day Augustine was in the city of Milan, Italy, with his books. He had become familiar, in his vast learning, with the epistles of Paul. He was seated in a garden when suddenly he heard a young child chanting a little jingle. The child was singing, "Take and read, take and read." Augustine took out Paul's epistle to the Romans and opened it up. He came to Romans 13:13–14, which says: "Let us behave properly as in the day, not in carousing and drunkenness, not in sexual promiscuity and sensuality, not in strife and jealousy. But put on the Lord Jesus Christ, and make no provision for the flesh in regard to its lusts."

Augustine, thirty-three years old at the time, was cut to the heart. Through the seeds planted by his Christian mother and through the power of God's Word—in particular the epistles of Paul—Augustine was converted to Jesus Christ. He committed himself wholly to a life of Christian service. In A.D. 395 he was appointed (despite his tears of protest that he was not worthy) as Bishop of Hippo.

Then in the year 410 a geopolitical cataclysm occurred. The pagan Visigoths had been driven from their Germanic homeland by the Huns. Booted out of their own land, the Visigoths went on the move, slaughtering and conquering as they went. They finally arrived at Rome, where, to the shock of the entire Roman Empire, the Roman army was unable to push them back. The Visigoths entered Rome—the city that had known peace and security for some two hundred years—and sacked it.

Refugees from Rome poured into the cities of North Africa to escape the pillage and death in Italy. They brought with them the stories of Rome's fall. To those who had grown up in the shadow of Roman domination, such a thing was unimaginable. They also brought with them a question: Would Rome have fallen if it had not neglected the traditional pagan gods and permitted this new Christian religion to flourish? *Surely if the Christian God was real,* they wondered, *would He not have protected them from these savage, invading barbarians?*

Augustine was so convinced that current events had presented a question that needed answering that he committed himself to addressing that question in his monumental work, *City of God.* In Augustine's writings we see the beginning point for Christians, in a post-first-century Church context, trying to work out the relationship between the Church and their secular state, between believers bound for a celestial city and the earthly community in which they must conduct their pilgrimage.

At the core of *City of God* are two cities: the City of God, and the city of man. The City of God is the eternal kingdom of Jesus Christ, while the city of man consists of the temporal kingdoms, cultures, and societies of this life. For Augustine the two cities, while different, are not hermetically sealed off from one another. Augustine points out that the present city of man is comprised of both sinners and saints—of those bound for the City of God and those bound for hell. The two kingdoms are "mixed" in this present epoch, before we are finally made part of God's eternal, heavenly city.[2]

How did Augustine, then, view the interaction between the believer and the fallen world?

In his thinking, the Christian possesses a spiritual peace from God but is also in need of the external peace that brings an orderly society. Even the unsaved sinner, according to Augustine, seeks this latter kind of peace. Thus, to this end, the Christian should pray and work toward maximizing peace, security, and good social order in the culture. At the same time, the believer knows that his is the work of a pilgrim whose ultimate destination is not found in this world but the next.

In support of this argument, Augustine rested his case on two verses from Scripture in particular. First, he cited 1 Timothy 2:2.[3] There Paul urged the benefits to believers of living in an environment of a peaceful life where devotion and love can flourish. Therefore, we should pray for our leaders. Why? In order that they will rule wisely and that the Church can flourish in an atmosphere of peace. At the time Paul wrote, Christians were excluded from any possibility of participatory democracy in the Roman Empire. Today, we can conclude that the principles of 1 Timothy 2:2 would be violated if we diligently prayed for good leaders, but did nothing to prevent bad ones from coming to power.

Second, Augustine referred to Jeremiah 29:7 in support of his argument. In that passage we see the children of Israel taken into political and religious bondage by the cruel and pagan culture of the Babylonian Empire. The Lord, through the prophet Jeremiah, advised them how to conduct themselves in the midst of their difficult situation. The children of God were told to "seek the welfare of the city where I have sent you into exile, and pray to the LORD on its behalf; for in its welfare you will have welfare."

This brilliant bishop noted that the city of God and the city of man were, for the present, "intermingled." Thus, he reasoned, "as long as the two cities are intermingled we also make use of the peace of Babylon." What is this "peace of Babylon"? To Augustine it meant "the temporal peace of the meantime, which is shared by good and bad alike."[4]

What is the practical effect of Augustine's overview of the role of the Christian in a fallen culture? What is the responsibility of the believer to work toward that "peace of Babylon?" We get a strong indication of this in his *City of God.* Augustine praised one emperor in particular who "never relaxed his endeavors to help the Church against the ungodly by just and compassionate legislation." In other words, when Christians exert godly influence toward "just and compassionate legislation" that seeks to protect and preserve the liberties of the Church, they are doing so in the best of Christian traditions.

Augustine urged Christians, nearly sixteen hundred years ago, to be able to discern the good ruler from the wicked one. What follows is his picture of the "happy [just and good] ruler." Considering the fact that God has granted Americans the great and awesome stewardship of actually electing our rulers—a privilege that neither Augustine nor his contemporaries had—this may be a good starting point to define the Christian standard of leadership for the twenty-first century:

> We Christians call rulers happy, if they rule with justice; if amid the voices of exalted praise and reverent salutations of excessive humility, they are not inflated with pride, but remember that they are but men; if they put their power at the service of God's majesty, to extend his worship far and wide; if they fear God, love him and worship him; if, more than their earthly kingdom, they love that realm where they do not fear to share the kingship. . . and if they do not fail to offer to their true God, as a sacrifice for their sins, the oblation of humility, compassion, and prayer."[5]

THE REFORMATION

It has been suggested recently that if evangelicals follow the example of the leaders of the Reformation, they will flee cultural battles at almost all costs. Luther and Calvin are cited for the proposition that the true calling of the Christian cannot be reconciled with the earthly pursuits of politics, and that those who are called to preach the gospel should avoid descending to this "lower kingdom" of "sounding brass and tinkling cymbal."[6]

This approach ignores the context and historical setting of the Reformers. These were not men who were recommending separation from a predominantly secular state (the kind of situation we have today). Instead, they were seeking protection from the over-reaching political *and* theological grip of the medieval Church. In other words, the Reformers wanted to insure the religious freedom of the evangelical believer from a state system whose theology was at odds with their view of Scripture.

The Reformation was, without question, a pivotal point of human history. One of the powerful aftershocks of this theological revolution was a shake-up of the millennia-old concept of the divine right of kings. In short, without the Reformation, it is doubtful whether democracy would ever have flourished.

This fact seems to be admitted even by those who hold great disdain for the accomplishments of the Reformers. Take, for instance, the comments of Charles Van Doren. His credentials are impressive: associate director of the Institute for Philosophical Research in Chicago, editor of numerous books on history, and holder of advanced degrees in both literature and mathematics. His observations on the Reformation, and Martin Luther in particular, are none too kind. Van Doren charges Luther with having initiated and supported the "intolerance" that swept violently through Europe, producing social mayhem and conflicts "almost as unhealthy as the Black Death," as "Protestants killed for their faith."[7]

Yet even Mr. Van Doren has to concede that with the new awareness of individual responsibility before God that accompanied the Reformation (rather than through blind obedience to Church hierarchy), was probably the very character trait "that makes good citizens in a democratic society."

Roland Bainton, an acknowledged expert on the Reformation, noted that the "claim that all of the religious contestants of the sixteenth century contributed to modern democracy at the point of denying state absolutism is incontestable."[8]

No matter what your personal political or cultural ideas, this much must be agreed: There is a critical connection between the

Reformation challenge to the way we view our relationship with God and the success of democracy in the modern world. The Christian gospel of grace, freedom, and individual moral responsibility paved the way for political and social liberty.

John Calvin has been given as an example of one who, as a leader of the Reformation, noted the basic difference between an earthly kingdom and Christ's spiritual kingdom, and urged that the two realms stay entirely separate. According to this line of argument, these two types of kingdoms should never be mixed together. In support of this position, Calvin's *Institutes* are cited.[9]

This argument misses the point. Calvin wanted to make sure that believers did not *confuse* the functions of the two kingdoms. But he certainly did not encourage Christians to retreat from the one in order to do the work of the other. Calvin's approach was antithetical to the monastic experience of spirituality characterized by the Middle Ages.

Moreover, Calvin actually illustrates the importance of Christians exerting influence on their political system. Take Calvin's monumentally important work, *The Institutes of the Christian Religion*, as an example. The *Institutes* are a strong argument for the need for believers to aggressively engage their culture, including their government. They were written by Calvin in 1536 as an open letter (so to speak) to the king of France. The *Institutes*, containing Calvin's declaration of his Christian theology, were penned in an effort to convince the ruling political system (i.e., the king) that Protestant followers of Calvin should be accorded equal protection of the law.

In his introduction to the *Institutes*, Calvin argues:

> But I plead the cause of all the godly, and consequently
> of Christ himself, which, having been in these times

persecuted and trampled on in all ways in your kingdom, now lies in a most deplorable state; and this indeed rather through the tyranny of certain Pharisees, than with your knowledge . . . For the ungodly have gone to such lengths that the truth of Christ, if not vanquished, dissipated, and entirely destroyed, is buried, as it were, in ignoble obscurity, while the poor, despised church is either destroyed by cruel massacres, or driven away into banishment, or menaced and terrified into total silence.[10]

Does Calvin sound like the kind of Reformer who advocated that we simply seek to evangelize our pagan culture and not soil ourselves by exerting influence on our political system? Calvin believed that "political institutions are the asylums of the Church in this life, though civil government is distinct from the spiritual kingdom of Christ, our Author, instructs us respecting it as a signal blessing from God."

According to Professor Bainton, all of the Reformers "insisted that the state might not constrain the true religion."[11] The famous *Institutes* are proof of this. They were Calvin's petition to the government of his day ("the asylum of the Church") for the protection of the religious freedom of Christians.

Following this logic, evangelicals who interact with their cultural and political environment in a way to exert influence for the protection of the rights of Christians are doing so in the best of Reformation traditions. The real question then becomes, How can we best secure civil freedom for the Church in the twenty-first century?

One alternative is to ignore the moral decay around us and almost exclusively resort to evangelism. Yet "evangelism" (defined in its most narrow terms) in itself, as we saw in Chapter 5, is no guarantee of social reformation. Do we really believe that a society that is permitted to devolve into a pagan meanness, valueless immorality, and a disregard for our spiritual heritage (by tearing down our cherished symbols) will best protect the interests of the Church? That kind of thinking not only defies logic, but it contradicts history.

Neither can we use Martin Luther as an example of retreat from cultural engagement. In his *Address to the Christian Nobility of the German Nation,* Luther addressed a litany of matters of public welfare and public morality that sound like a position paper from the Moral Majority. He urged the reading of Scripture in the schools. Luther also argued that the authorities should find a way to outlaw houses of prostitution.

He recommended the outlawing of public begging and suggested that the authorities establish an official means to determine individual poverty and then lend assistance. Of course, throughout, Luther pleaded the cause of religious liberty for Christians. His point, he said, was "to show how much good temporal authority (human government) might do, and what should be the duty of all authorities."[12]

Although Luther believed that the kingdom of God and the kingdoms of man were separate entities, he also believed, as did his predecessor Augustine, that for the present time the "tares and the grain" were mixed. Thus, the state (which had the coercive power of the law) would mix with, and interact with, the church (whose real power was one of moral and spiritual influence). He was clearly opposed to the Church being instituted as a power of the state, and he was adamant that the state should have no power over the theological teachings of the Church. But between those twin peaks is a wide plain that needs to be occupied. Although Martin Luther was no political philosopher, it would appear he believed that Christians must plead, as effectively as possible, the cause of the protection of Church liberty, and that we should advocate the basics of public morals and the general welfare.

The Reformers never advanced the separatist idea of Christian retreat from culture. At the same time, however, they never did set forth a systematic strategy for followers of Christ to impact the state. They were too busy marshalling the creation of a new corporate identity for believers in the face of persecution and tyranny.

Later, we see the practical beginnings of such a strategy. In England, and even more clearly in the movement toward independence in America, the interaction between evangelical Christianity and the idea of self-governance came into sharper focus. The powerful new challenge of the Christian's responsibility as both citizen of heaven and citizen of a politically free nation was for the first time in human history waiting at the threshold. In the seventeenth century this challenge became a reality.

9 The Spirit of Liberty and the End of Kings

WHEN JANET AND I first moved to the Washington, D.C. area, we drove down Constitution Avenue in our nation's capital, taking in the buildings and monuments. We caught sight of one small memorial that made a deep impression on us. It was a statue of Nathan Hale, located outside the Department of Justice building. There he stood in bronze, his young head erect, a noose around his neck, uttering those famous words: "I only regret that I have but one life to lose for my country."

Hale was only twenty-one when he was executed in late September 1776. He had volunteered, at the request of General Washington, to cross enemy lines as a spy and determine the military positions of the British. He was caught and promptly hanged. Hale died with such courage that the British tried to keep the story of his death a secret, for fear that the example of that kind of bravery in such a young man might incite the American colonists to even greater resolve to win the war.

What was amazing to us is that this young man—who had earned a reputation as an excellent athlete and a gifted student at Yale—had his whole life ahead of him. Yet he sacrificed it all for a country that was less than three months old.

Great causes—like independence—require great sacrifices. Those who spearheaded the Reformation also had to take those kinds of risks. Some paid the ultimate price. As the Reformation idea caught fire, however, it helped spawn new ideas about freedom and about slavery—and about the obligations of the individual Christian as an earthly citizen while traveling on the pilgrimage to the Celestial City.

BLOOD AND FIRE: THE GOSPEL IS PREACHED

In the years after 1517, the momentous date when Luther had nailed his ninety-five theses to the church door at Wittenberg, Germany, followers of the Reformation began organizing in England. A young man named William Tyndale met with a group of Reformation Christians. The group would slip in the rear door of the White Horse Tavern at Cambridge to discuss the writings of the Reformers and to study the Bible. Tyndale was greatly influenced by Luther's German translation of the New Testament and felt pressed to begin his own translation in English. But when he traveled to London in the summer of 1523 in an effort to find support for the project, he was turned down by the newly appointed bishop there. Convinced that he would have to travel to the European continent in order to accomplish his translation, Tyndale sailed from England in the spring of 1524, never to return.

In the ensuing years William Tyndale translated both the New Testament and portions of the Old Testament; his work later formed the basis of the Authorized and Revised versions of the Bible. But the fires of persecution were always smoldering around him. Finally, in 1535, his enemies kidnapped him and dragged him off to the fortress of Vilvorde a few miles from Brussels. There he was imprisoned on the charge of heresy. Thomas Cromwell, the influential secretary of state for Henry VIII, made an impassioned diplomatic attempt to secure Tyndale's release, but without success. Because of his work in making the Scriptures available to the English-reading public, Tyndale was found guilty in the court of Charles V, and on October 6, 1536, he was tied to a stake to be burned alive as a heretic. The executioner apparently took pity on him and strangled him to death before the flames had a chance to reach him.

By the time Tyndale gave his last, and full measure, of sacrifice for the gospel, the Coverdale's Bible, which drew upon Tyndale's translation, was already being circulated throughout England with the permission of King Henry VIII.

Persecution continued to spread across Europe against this "heresy" of gospel faith. In 1562 the duke of Guise, on his way to Paris, led a charge against a large group of Reformation sympathizers while they were worshipping in Vassy, a town in the Champagne region. Over one hundred Protestants were either killed or seriously wounded; the duke was later assassinated by a Protestant protestor. Elsewhere, in the Netherlands, local religious inquisitions were used in an attempt to crush Lutheranism and Calvinism.

Meanwhile, in Scotland a furious outbreak of persecution against gospel believers had ensued. Patrick Hamilton, a young college student at St. Andrews University, became the first martyr for the Reformation gospel in Scotland. He had studied under Luther and then returned to Scotland, preaching and sharing the good news of salvation by grace through faith as well as the notion that Scripture, and Scripture alone, was the primary guide to faith and conduct. Hamilton was arrested in St. Andrews and burned at the stake at a spot on the sidewalk outside the aged and blackened walls of the university. The spot where he died is still marked by his initials fashioned in the bricks.

Twenty-eight years later Scottish preacher George Wishart, in a wave of persecution, was also burned at the stake just a few blocks away. Wishart's spiritual apprentice, John Knox, was captured and sentenced to serve as a rowing slave, chained to the bottom of a French galley ship.

It was against this backdrop of religious persecution by tyrannical rulers that a Scottish minister and theologian named Samuel Rutherford wrote a groundbreaking treatise, one hundred years later, called *Lex Rex*. The premise of Rutherford's work was simple enough. Stated plainly, he argued that the law is greater than the king. Freedom is best secured under a system of laws, Rutherford said, rather than by the whims of men whose right to rule is on the sole basis of bloodline. But because the prevailing notion in Europe and Great Britain had been that the governing of nations was the particular "divine right of kings," *Lex Rex* caused a sensation.

At that time, the Scottish Parliament was sympathetic to the restoration of Charles II to the throne. It was violently opposed to Protestantism, and outlawed its practices and persecuted its followers. Parliament ordered that *Lex Rex* be burned across the land, and anyone found in possession of the book was deemed to be an enemy of the government. Samuel Rutherford was placed under house arrest and scheduled to appear before the Parliament at Edinburgh to face the charge of high treason. However, at the age of sixty-one, his health was failing, and he died of natural causes before his opponents had the chance to convict and execute him (as they surely would have done). Samuel Rutherford's last words were "Glory, glory, dwelleth in

Emmanuel's land." The Scottish reformer who had challenged the absolute sovereignty of human kings was now entering the gates of the City of God.

Rooted in his understanding of the Bible and energized by the liberty of the gospel, Rutherford had championed the idea that Christians had a duty to fight for those freedoms that would more adequately insure the security of the Church and the protection of believers. He stated:

> The law of God, commanding that we love our neighbor as ourselves, and therefore to defend one another against unjust violence . . . obligeth us to the same, except we think God can be pleased with lip-love in love only, which the Spirit of God condemneth (1 John ii, 9, 10; iii, 16). And the sum of law and prophets is, that as we would not men should refuse to help us when we are unjustly oppressed, so neither would we so serve our afflicted brethren.[1]

Throughout *Lex Rex* Rutherford balanced the twin truths of the Christian's walk in the world: (1) that all government and the idea of an ordered society is from God, and (2) that as those who are called to act for the good of our neighbors, particularly those of the household of faith, we are called upon to do more than express "lip-love," as he expressed in his archaic English. Our actions must be motivated by the love of Christ and be bold in defense of the "unjustly oppressed" and "our afflicted brethren."

While we might debate the fine points of some of Rutherford's exposition of the obligation of Christians to overthrow tyrants, one thing is clear: he helped settle the question of whether the millennia-old practice of the arbitrary rule of monarchs was God's *primary* or even *preferred* system of governance.

His argument that God designed governments and rulers for the *general* protection of mankind, while at the same time opposing those *particular* rulers or systems involved in grotesque oppression and destruction, helped pave the way for the demise of the notion of the divine right of kings.

We are the beneficiaries of the dual zeal of men like William Tyndale, who spread the Word of God in the face of awesome persecution, and like Samuel Rutherford, who dared to suggest that God's design for government does not insure His divine approval of tyrants. Because of their inspiration and sacrifice, America and other freedom-loving nations were born.

What a travesty it would be to suggest that their sacrifices and their vision for freedom are no longer necessary. Because we are not ruled by kings of whimsy and caprice, and because martyrs are not burned in the streets, are we so different from them? We are, at any one time, merely one generation away from oppression and chaos. Liberty is best guarded with vigilance as well as sacrifice. Those virtues were in demand when our thirteen colonies fought for independence from the king of England. Yet the American Revolution was also fueled by a spiritual understanding of individual freedom before God that was distinctly Christian and thoroughly biblical.

A FEW GREAT FALLACIES ABOUT OUR FIGHT FOR FREEDOM

Those who look for the secular roots of the American Revolution often look to such things as the Boston Tea Party or the Boston Massacre as great singular, precipitating events. In a broad sense, an explanation for the push for American independence is often seen in economic terms. As a people, we were primarily seeking economic power, according to some scholars of American history.

Yet the idea that the American Revolution was primarily a financial feud masterminded by rich land-owning gentry who wanted to preserve their way of life is an outlandish suggestion. That notion is as inaccurate as an anti-American cartoon that appeared in the British press in 1780. At that time England was knee-deep in the war with the colonies. Samuel Adams, perceived as one of the primary American agitators for the war for colonial independence, was lampooned in a British picture that portraying him as a rich nobleman relaxing in his palatial drawing room overlooking a vast estate. The cartoon, which was pure propaganda, was ridiculously inaccurate. Samuel Adams was actually so poor that his friends had to buy him a suit to wear to the Continental Congress.[2]

When, in explaining the origins of the American Revolution, historians go beyond the obvious explanations—like King George's notoriously bad political judgment, or the anger of independent-minded and stubborn colonialists, or speculations about the economic motivations of that time—they still often miss the mark. When a search for the ideological roots of the Revolution is launched, the boat of modern scholarship often lands squarely at the port of Enlightenment and rationalistic thinking of such godless men as Montesquieu or Voltaire. Typical of this approach is the Pulitzer prize-winning work by historian Bernard Bailyn. He concludes that:

> More directly influential in shaping the thought of the Revolutionary generation were the ideas and attitudes associated with the writings of the Enlightenment rationalism—writings that expressed not simply the rationalism of liberal reform but that of enlightened conservatism as well.[3]

Harvard professor Bailyn praises the "writings of the Enlightenment rationalism," but he totally ignores the massive contribution of a purely evangelical phenomenon that immediately preceded the move for American independence. This historical epoch of spiritual revival in the early 1700s, conveniently overlooked by politically correct historians, was one of the true catalysts for America's fight for freedom.

THE GREAT AWAKENING

Gospel revival in the eighteenth century really began in England. The preaching of John and Charles Wesley and George Whitefield pressed not only for the need for individual salvation and conversion through acceptance of and faith in Jesus Christ, but also for the need for personal moral purity and holiness in a life of joyful service to the Lord. Whitefield preached a particularly powerful but simple gospel message.

In 1738 he came to the American colonies and began a traveling evangelistic ministry in Georgia and New England. John Wesley also came across the Atlantic to the colonies to preach. Whitefield was succeeded by John Davenport, a Yale student from Long Island. Davenport carried on large open-air evangelistic meetings throughout New England. Revival swept through the colonies, down through Anglican-controlled Virginia where, particularly in the Piedmont regions, the "new birth" was being claimed by scores of new believers in Christ.

The Great Awakening, as this revival was later called, was not a mere emotional response to gospel conversion. Though some undoubtedly made professions of faith for less than sincere reasons, the movement as a whole was thoroughly evangelical and spiritually authentic. During this time the brilliant early American preacher Jonathan Edwards, from his pulpit in Massachusetts and throughout his writings, helped provide the theological underpinnings for the evangelicalism sweeping the nation.

The effect of the Great Awakening on the American people was profound. But it was particularly timely in preparing the hearts of believers for understanding liberty, in the same way that the Reformation had kindled the idea of freedom and contributed to the collapse of the medieval monarchies. Historian Paul Johnson noted:

> The Great Awakening was the proto-revolutionary event, the formative moment in American history, preceding the political drive for independence and making it possible . . . Its key text was Revelation 21:5: "Behold, I make all things new"—which was also the text for the American experience as a whole.[4]

While politically correct histories of America specialize in expunging this colossal evangelistic phenomena from the landscape, the fact is that "the Revolution could not have taken place without this religious background . . . the American Revolution, in its origins, was a religious event . . ."[5]

The point of the Great Awakening and its causal contribution to the American Revolution is that the evangelical understanding of the gospel has, throughout history, been a contributing factor to a new, and sometimes radical, understanding of how our nations should be run. When God penetrates our hearts with His light and opens our eyes to His Word, that becomes the preeminent guiding event. Is it logical to believe, then, that we should (or even can) fail to take that preeminent guiding event along with us into our involvement in the public affairs of the day—into the local school board, or the town council, or the state house, or the Congress?

When men and women experience the new birth in Christ and look to the Scriptures for guidance on how to conduct themselves in the world, they have consistently sought to influence their cultures and their communities in matters of human relationships, politics, charity, and social mores. To suggest that twenty-first-century Christians need to substantially recalibrate the extent to which they intermingle with the politics of their culture is to deny the force of two thousand years of history. It also ignores the particular place that the Christian gospel has earned in influencing the American idea of liberty from the very inception of this nation.

CHRISTIANITY AND THE LIBERTY BELL

Christianity and the influence of the Church were integral factors in the American Revolution. From the pulpits of colonial churches, and particularly those in New England, a Christian exposition of liberty, citizenship, and political duty went forth regularly in the years leading up to the fight for American independence. In fact, such preachers have been dubbed the forgotten heroes of the Revolution.[6] They regularly delivered election-day sermons in the decade before 1776, urging citizens to do their civic duty and thereby realize their duty to God. Typical of such sentiments were the words of Reverend Charles Turner of Duxbury, Massachusetts. Two years before the Declaration of Independence, he preached that "religious liberty is so blended with civil, that if one falls it is not expected that the other will continue."[7] In another election-day sermon, Reverend William Gordon urged Christians to offer practical assistance in the fight for independence that seemed to loom ever closer on the horizon:

There is not an individual but may be aiding and assisting to the common cause one way or another . . . The
godly by their inwrought, fervent prayers, which avail
much with their heavenly Father. The martial and courageous by their personal bravery. The timid by concealing
their fears . . . the poor may assist by determining that tho'
poor they will be free; and that if they cannot have riches,
they will not wear chains.[8]

This influence of Christianity continued through the Revolution and into the founding and expansion of America. John
Witherspoon, a former evangelical Scottish pastor and president
of New Jersey College (later renamed Princeton), single-handedly wielded a tremendous influence over the direction of
American government. He taught James Madison the Calvinis-
tic view of the inherent sin nature of man—a view that would
later form the basis of Madison's design, as the architect of the
Constitution, of our particular form of government. Three separate and coequal branches of government were established, lest
any one branch become too powerful as a result of the sinful
tendencies of human leaders.

Witherspoon expounded, like many other preachers of the
day, on the interdependence of religious freedom and civil freedom. His influence on America's direction would have been
substantial had he just limited his activities to his college: his
students later became state governors, U.S. senators and con-
gressmen, cabinet members, Supreme Court justices, and one
became vice president. James Madison, who first considered
entering the Christian ministry while attending Witherspoon's
school, would later become president of the United States.

Yet Witherspoon's sense of civic calling went far beyond the green lawns of New Jersey College. He served on the Continental Congress and was the only preacher to sign the Declaration of Independence. After America won her independence, Witherspoon served several terms in the New Jersey legislature and led the fight to outlaw the slave trade in that state.

After the initial Articles of Confederation proved too frail to hold the American union together, a Constitution was drafted in 1787 and ratified by the states the next year. In 1789 Congress convened and approved the amendments to the Constitution, including the First Amendment, which guaranteed religious liberty. According to newspaper accounts of the day, Madison, the chief draftsman, had promised friends in Virginia that his first priority would be the passage of a constitutional amendment protecting freedom of religion.

One of the first orders of business for Congress, in 1789, was to pass a measure providing for the payment of a salary for the chaplain of the Congress, who would conduct opening prayers. Three days later, the same men approved the language of the First Amendment. It is obvious that they had no flights of fancy about the kind of absolute "wall of separation" between church and state imbedded in the thinking of our current courts.

When President George Washington resigned his commission as commander in chief of the revolutionary army, he circulated his farewell message to the governors of the thirteen states. He ended it with his "earnest prayer," that they remember: "what doth the Lord require of thee, but to do justly, and to l ove mercy, and to walk humbly with thy God," quoting from Micah 6:8. He expressed, in this farewell address, the belief that the only possibility for a "happy nation" lay in our adopting the characteristics of Jesus Christ.[9] Thirteen years later, when he gave his farewell address after serving as president of the United

States, Washington returned to the same theme, proclaiming that there was no chance of any successful national morality—indeed, no hope for any real civic virtue at all—apart from the primary source of morality, which is found in our worship of God.

John Adams, one of the pioneers of the movement for American independence and later a president himself (and the father of John Quincy Adams, who also became president), once wrote in his twilight years that there were two principles which knit the nation together during the Revolution: the ideas of English and American liberty, and the general principles of Christianity.

While president, James Madison signed a bill into law that aided the Bible society in distributing Scripture. He also issued proclamations for official days of fasting, prayer, and thanksgiving to God.

While Thomas Jefferson is often cited by secularists as someone who would have approved our contemporary hostility toward expressions of belief in God in the public sphere, his actions do not bear this out. As the founder of the University of Virginia (a public university), he voiced no objections over its earliest commencement exercises, which included prayer and religious invocations.

Those who wring their hands over the involvement of the Christian church in culture, public affairs, and government ignore the history of our nation. It is interesting that one of the most astute observers of the intimate relationship between the church and our public institutions in America was not, himself, an American. Alexis de Tocqueville was an assistant magistrate in France. He was appointed to travel to our nation in 1831 to study our prison system. While traversing America he recorded his observations about American life, politics, culture, and manners in his journal, which would later be published as *Democracy in America.*

Tocqueville noted that while "religion in America takes no direct part in the government of society . . . it must be regarded as the first of [America's] institutions . . . I am certain that they hold it to be indispensable to the maintenance of republican institutions." He also wrote:

> The Americans combine the notions of Christianity and of liberty so intimately in their minds that it is impossible to make them conceive the one without the other; and with them this conviction does not spring from that barren, traditionary faith which seems to vegetate rather than to live in the soul.
>
> . . . Thus religious zeal is perpetually warmed in the United States by the fires of patriotism.[10]

It is simply the blunt lesson of history that if the current mindset of secularism had reigned during the founding years of America, and if the Christian church had not been our preeminent moral influence, one of two things would have happened: either we would never have survived as a nation; or, equally troubling, we would not be free.

10 From Old Evils to the New Millennium

THE TWO OF us have accumulated a substantial pile of press releases and bulletins over the years from groups like Planned Parenthood, National Organization for Women, and ACLU. These publications have two common threads. First, they paint conservative Christians as the enemies of constitutional government and opponents of freedom. Second, they paint themselves (they are, by and large, secularists who do not accept the authority of the Bible or the ideas of Christian orthodoxy) as the champions of the moral high ground.

This latter point is ironic and incorrect. When you review the last 150 years in England and America, evangelical Christians were at the forefront of the great moral issues of the day. History has proven that evangelicals stood for the right, the true, and the just, in the face of a culture holding on desperately to old forms of institutionalized evil. One such evil was slavery.

SLAVE BOATS AND PARLIAMENT VOTES

From the mid-eighteenth century to the mid-nineteenth century, political ties between the American colonies and Great

Britain were consistently strained. They were torn apart on a hot July day in Philadelphia, in 1776. With the Declaration of Independence the Colonies were plunged into a war for independence that even General Washington feared we might not be able to win. Even after defeating the British in a series of decisive battles in 1781, and after negotiating a peace treaty that recognized American sovereignty in 1782, our nation again found itself at war with England in 1812.

The war was spawned, in part because of disputes over control of Canada and arose out of ongoing naval battles between the two nations. America found itself initially humiliated when British troops invaded the city of Washington on August 24, 1812. President James Madison fled the capital. His wife, First Lady Dolly Madison, had to disguise herself and seek refuge in the streets. She was actually refused entrance at the first inn she reached in her attempt to find safety. The Capitol was set on fire, along with the U.S. Treasury. Ultimately America prevailed with the help of Major General Andrew Jackson. He was a fierce and unyielding military commander who led scruffy frontiersmen-turned-soldiers like Davy Crockett and Sam Houston into battle against the British and the Creek Indian Nation, whom England had maliciously enlisted and armed against the Americans.

Despite these turbulent political disruptions between America and Britain, these two nations shared, even during these times, two intriguing spiritual connections. The first was the Great Awakening, as we have already seen. Spiritual revival on American shores in the 1700s originated, at least in great part, in the preaching of British evangelists who traveled from England, where the revival had started, across the Atlantic to our shores.

The second spiritual bond was the similar role of evangelicalism in both countries in efforts to eradicate the slave trade. In both England and America the struggle to ban slavery and emancipate slaves bore the marks of a distinctly Christian form of activism.

John Wesley, a prominent English evangelist and preacher, consistently and clearly denounced the practice of slavery from his pulpit. In a village south of London known as Clapham, a group of committed Christian believers who had been gathering together for worship, Bible study, and social action forged an antislavery alliance that would change history. The Clapham Sect, as they were later called, included men of tremendous influence in England. There was Henry Thorton, a Member of Parliament (MP) and wealthy financier; Charles Grant, chairman of the East India Company; James Stephen, a famous English barrister; and Zachary Macaulay, a former governor of English-controlled Sierra Leone.[1]

Perhaps the best-known person in the group was William Wilberforce, an MP considered to be one of the greatest living orators in England at the time. History would later show that he played a major role in accomplishing the eradication of the British slave trade.

Wilberforce was converted to Jesus Christ in 1784. Though he continued to serve in Parliament, before long he began to consider leaving politics altogether. Wilberforce entertained the idea of taking his Holy Orders and entering the ministry. However, he did not do so, primarily because of the urging of John Newton, a former slave-ship captain who was won to Christ and later became a pastor and renowned hymn writer.

Newton's spiritual birth is a remarkable story in itself. He had been born into a seafaring family. At twenty-three he was a captain of a slave ship and an atheist with a reputation for outrageous blasphemy. On March 10, 1748, after a terrifying ocean storm, and after reading Thomas à Kempis's *The Imitation of Christ,* he gave his life to Christ. Newton gave up the slave trade, married, settled down, and came under the influence of several leaders of the evangelical revival in England, including Charles Wesley and George Whitefield. In 1764 he was ordained into the ministry. Newton later penned "Amazing Grace" and numerous other powerful hymns.

It was Newton, a pastor, who suggested to Wilberforce that he could serve God best not in the pulpit but in the well of debate on the floor of Parliament. Newton advised Wilberforce that in order to accomplish the complete eradication of slavery, such an undertaking called out for the service of a committed Christian statesman to captain it to its God-willed destination. William Wilberforce, as the aged pastor saw it, was clearly such a man.

The political battle to banish slavery was hard and often bitter. Wilberforce and his Christian compatriots were vehemently opposed by English merchants and financiers who profited by the slave trade that tilled the soil of British territories. The anti-slavery Christians were opposed by British naval hero Admiral Nelson and even by King George III, who considered the Clapham Sect a group of dangerous revolutionaries. Starting in 1788, Wilberforce and the Clapham Christians worked for nineteen years to outlaw the slave trade. The bill for the banning of slave trading on English lands was introduced and defeated eleven times before victory was finally achieved. But even when that bill was finally passed by Parliament, slaves then located in British territories were still considered the property of slave owners. Just the *sale and trading* of slaves had been outlawed. It took another twenty-six years for all slaves on English lands to be emancipated. This was finally secured in 1833, at the time of William Wilberforce's death.

Wilberforce and the Clapham Christians are testimony to how, when godly men and women respond to the call of God, they can help eradicate the scourge of evil from the land. But they are also testimony to the *manner* in which Christians must wage such battles. In London's Westminster Abbey, amid the busts of great writers like Shakespeare, and surrounded by the tombs of once powerful kings and queens of England, there is a memorial to William Wilberforce. It was his Christian life, the inscription states, for which he will be primarily remembered. This is the legacy Christians must leave in our nation as we enter the twenty-first century. Though we may wage fierce battles for the souls of our citizens and for the moral survival of our nation, may we be remembered for the fact that our Christian walk matched our Christian witness.

THE SCOPES TRIAL:
MAKING MONKEYS OUT OF THE CONSERVATIVE CHURCH

By 1800 a Second Great Awakening was sweeping through New England into the South and the Western territories. Congregational, Baptist, and Methodist churches were ignited with the fires of revival. Charles Finney, a former trial lawyer who became a full-time evangelist after coming to Christ in 1821, began conducting preaching tours across the nation. The mid-1800s saw spontaneous prayer meetings spring up, and there was a dramatic surge in church attendance across the country.

While the slavery issue caused a bitter division in America halfway through the century, the leading edge of the slavery abolition movement was headed by gospel-preaching, evangelical Christians, as we document in Chapter 15. The nineteenth century also saw the creation of numerous Christian colleges, seminaries, missionary societies, hospitals, and other charities and benevolent groups for the spread of the gospel, for the care of the needy, and for the improvement of public morals. Groups like the American Bible Society, the American Sunday School Union, the American Tract Society in America, and the Salvation Army in England were all founded in the 1800s.

By the end of the century, though, there was also a growing intellectual movement openly hostile to biblical Christianity. In Europe the psychoanalytical theories of Freud were taking root, and human behavior was viewed not as our freely chosen actions to sin or not sin in a universe created by a moral God, but was instead explained on the basis of subliminal psychological motivations. At the same time, the ideas of philosophers like Friedrich Nietzsche were causing great excitement in Germany. Nietzsche denounced the existence of God and worshipped at the secular altar of human self-determination and self-will.

In the religion arena there was a rising tide of theological modernism. Radical theologians were gaining influence under their banner of so-called "higher criticism"—a euphemism for taking a low view of Scripture and denying all things miraculous or supernatural in the Bible, while at the same time taking a high view of human reason and science in interpreting God's Word. The new social sciences treated the development of Christianity simply as an inevitable step in the social evolution of our ancient predecessors rather than as a body of revealed truth about who God is and how we are to relate to Him through His Son.

In response, the modern Christian fundamentalist movement was birthed. In 1919 the World's Christian Fundamentals Association held its first conference, at which they reaffirmed the fundamentals of Christianity and took aim at theological modernism. Conservative Protestant leaders adhered to five main theological points: (1) the verbal inerrancy and inspiration of Scripture; (2) the deity of Jesus Christ; (3) the virgin birth; (4) the substitutionary atonement for sin, accomplished by Christ in His death on the cross; and (5) the bodily resurrection of Jesus and His bodily return at some point in the future.

To most of us now, these principles are not surprising—indeed, they comprise the mainstay of the Christian faith. However, the cultural opponents to fundamentalism have successfully painted that movement as something radical, sinister, and backward. How this was accomplished involves, in great part, the cultural and legal battle known as the Scopes trial in Dayton, Tennessee. That case has been seized upon by liberal forces to rewrite the historical record and turn the debate over the teaching of evolution into a witchhunt against fundamentalism.

One of the most powerful anti-Christian weapons in the last half of the nineteenth century was provided by Charles Darwin and his theory of biological evolution. While he was not the first one to come up with the concept of evolution of the species, his singular contribution was providing a theory for the supposed *means* by which evolution was to have been accomplished. While crisscrossing the oceans of the globe on a five-year study of nature aboard the *H.M.S. Beagle*, Darwin postulated the theory of natural selection—popularly known as "survival of the fittest." This concept was integrated into several other humanistic philosophical systems—including Karl Marx's use of it in developing his idea of the class struggle in history, which was his theoretical basis for communism. Ideas of "social Darwinism" have also been linked to the ultimate rise of Nazism in twentieth-century Germany.

Christian leaders in the early part of the 1900s rightly recognized the threat of scientific and philosophical modernism, and particularly the antagonism of Darwin's theories to biblical Christianity. However, there is a lesson to be learned from the ensuing battle that took place between Christian fundamentalists and evolutionists: It is not sufficient to merely recognize the intellectual threats to gospel truth and then wade into the cultural battle, if the battle plan is not well thought out and wisely implemented. The biblical admonition to be "shrewd as serpents and innocent as doves" (Matt. 10:16) certainly should have applied to the battle against evolution.

Shortly after the turn of the century, the evolution-creation debate had broken out across college and university campuses as well as the popular lecture circuit. In his detailed telling of the background of the Scopes trial, law professor Edward Larson points out that several initial attempts at legislation on the evolution issue, supported by fundamentalists, were unsuccessful. In Kentucky an antievolution bill died in 1922 without passage. Out of the six states that considered legislation prohibiting the teaching of evolution in 1923, most failed. Oklahoma passed a restriction on the purchase of textbooks teaching Darwinian evolution, and Florida passed a nonbinding resolution on the subject.[2]

One of the chief national spokesmen for the pro-creation viewpoint was William Jennings Bryan. However, Bryan's position was balanced by several well-reasoned considerations. First, he made it clear that his objection was "not to teaching the evolutionary hypothesis as a hypothesis, but to the teaching of it as true or as a proven fact."[3] Second, Bryan urged state legislators, in crafting language for antievolution bills, to avoid making the teaching of evolution a criminal offense or making it subject to fine or punishment. Third, Bryan did not try to make his case for antievolution laws on the basis of trying to replace science with the Bible. Rather, he argued that when the taxpayers pay for public education, they have the right to dictate what is taught in the curriculum. One of his speeches actually suggested an argument for balanced treatment—that it would be unfair to permit evolution to be taught and not to also permit a creationist view of the universe at the same time.

However, Tennessee legislators ignored Bryan's approach and passed a law that made it a crime to teach man's evolution from the "lower order of animals" and to deny the creation story "as taught in the Bible." That would prove to be a major mistake of public policy as well as an error of apologetic strategy for conservative Christians. Waiting in the wings were liberal secularists—rabid opponents of all things biblical and particularly fundamentalist—who were looking both for a test case and for a teacher-as-martyr-for-academic-freedom to be their client. The state of Tennessee, when it passed this legislation, handed the test case over to the ACLU on a silver platter.

The teacher-martyr was not hard to find. The ACLU was looking for a case to put it into the national spotlight. In a bizarre collaboration with the ACLU, Dayton, Tennessee officials actually encouraged (if not actually staged) the prosecution of a teacher named John Scopes for teaching evolution. The ACLU offered to pay for the costs of the prosecution so it could have the privilege of defending the case. Scopes was not even the regular biology teacher. He was the football coach and a general science instructor. However, he had been substituting for the regular biology teacher, and had been using, quite unwittingly, a state-approved textbook that violated the newly enacted state law. After being approached, he agreed to be the defendant in a test case. Scopes had little to lose. The ACLU would handle all of his expenses, and he was not married, had no family ties to Dayton, and had little intention of staying there anyway.

The actual conduct of the Scopes trial, while fascinating, is nearly irrelevant compared to the impact of the trial on the ensuing cultural portrayal of Christian fundamentalists. As a result of the trial, Scopes was convicted by a jury and ordered to pay a nominal fine. On appeal the ACLU was successful in reversing the conviction in the Tennessee Supreme Court, but not on the broad academic freedom grounds they wished. After the case went back to the lower court, the Dayton officials declined to reprosecute, and the case died a quiet death.

The cast of characters in the case was important. Scopes was defended by Clarence Darrow, lead defense counsel of a group of renowned trial lawyers. Darrow was the most famous criminal defense lawyer of his day and a hardened agnostic/atheist. He had been raised by a father who was an active socialist and vehemently opposed the ideas of organized religion. He did not accept the case in order to battle for lofty constitutional values; Darrow's motives were much more blunt. The case would, in addition to placing him in the national limelight, afford him the opportunity to bash Christian fundamentalists. As he left for Dayton, Darrow told reporters he was looking for a victory in the case whereby America would reject the "narrow, mean, intolerable and brainless prejudice of soul-less religio-manics."[4] He was referring to Christian fundamentalists, particularly, his opposing counsel, William Jennings Bryan. Darrow made it clear that his main goal was to expose the political agenda of Christian fundamentalists.

In the historical retelling of the Scopes trial, American liberalism has enjoyed a revisionism and distortion unparalleled in modern times. The main ammunition for this assault came from the Broadway play *Inherit the Wind*, produced in 1955. The underlying target of the play was really the recent battle in the 1950s with McCarthyism, as both the playwrights and actor Tony Randall (who starred in the original production) stated in interviews at the time.[5] Christian fundamentalists in the play proved to be useful images, portrayed as the tyrants over the mind of America. Bryan was pictured as a pompous ignoramus and a right-wing Christian.

In fact, Bryan was a progressive in his politics, and ran for president on the Democratic ticket. He shared the Democratic Party in common with Darrow, who had an unsuccessful run for Congress as a Democrat. Bryan's support of women's suffrage and his opposition to war would probably make him look like a moderate or liberal today.

It would be dangerous to underestimate the propaganda effect of the retelling of the Scopes trial via *Inherit the Wind*, particularly after it was turned into a movie starring Hollywood luminaries Spencer Tracy and Frederick March. The Scopes trial continues to haunt the cultural scene to this day.

When in *Epperson v. Arkansas* the Supreme Court struck down an Arkansas law that prohibited the teaching of evolution (it was passed in the wake of the Scopes trial but never enforced), references to *Scopes v. Tennessee* littered the lower court record and the popular media accounts. By the time "balanced treatment" laws from Louisiana were challenged in the Supreme Court many years later, the intellectual battle over whether creation deserved equal time in the marketplace of ideas had already been lost in the institutions of the elite culture. Even though the vast majority of Americans favored equal treatment of creationism at a minimum, universities balked at giving creationists equal academic freedom; the media trumpeted the bugle of another "Scopes" case, and the Supreme Court saw the law as an unconstitutional establishment of the religion. In *Edwards v. Aguillard*

Justice Brennan, writing for the majority in striking down the Louisiana law, made reference to the Scopes case.

The saga still continues. In 1998 Craig took the case of a tenured public university professor and argued it before the Third Circuit Court of Appeals in Philadelphia. At issue was a ban placed on the professor (because he was perceived to be a "fundamentalist") prohibiting him from lecturing from a long list of materials deemed to be unduly "religious." Among the materials banned was information on the creation-evolution debate. The professor wanted to enlighten his university students (they were in the education department, and therefore would be future teachers) on this curriculum battle that continues in public schools across the nation.

The Court of Appeals indicated that it had little sympathy for the way in which the university had treated one of its distinguished professors. However, the Court ruled that under the present state of the law, a public university has nearly absolute authority to determine its own curriculum and to censor its professors from deviating, even if its policy is motivated by anti-Christian bigotry. In 1999 the U.S. Supreme Court turned down Craig's petition for certiorari in the case, though it was urged to take up the case by a prestigious academic freedom foundation.

In just a few decades since the battle of William Jennings Bryan and Clarence Darrow in a Tennessee courtroom, the battle over evolution has come full circle. Today Christian scholars face a real-life version of the kind of discrimination that liberalism could only fancifully invent in the John Scopes case. The difference today is that the ACLU, the courts, and the media have apparently lined up on the side of the censors and the bigots. It is utterly naive to think that this situation will simply right itself with time. Christians need to continue taking concerted, decisive, and strategic action on the issue of Christian discrimination. If we do not, America will begin looking like the reverse of Darwin's evolutionary theory: our nation will devolve from a society of equally free citizens into something resembling the planet of the apes.

THE CHURCH IN THE LAST QUARTER OF THE TWENTIETH CENTURY

Since the 1970s and early 1980s, evangelical Christians have given concerted effort to organizing and engaging in the cultural and moral battles. As a result, we have seen the creation of numerous national groups, formed from a Judeo-Christian worldview, which have pledged to change the moral, spiritual, political, and legal climate in America.

What is consistent among them is that they were founded by leaders who felt called by God to energize Christians and pro-family citizens to effect change for the better. Jerry Falwell with the Moral Majority; Pat Robertson with the Christian Coalition and the American Center for Law and Justice; John Whitehead with The Rutherford Institute; Beverly LaHaye with Concerned Women for America; Gary Bauer with the Family Research Institute; and Don Wildmon with the American Family Association are just a few.

The question has been raised whether these large-scale efforts by the evangelical church have been misguided. *Christianity Today* posed that question to Jerry Falwell recently. The cover of that issue summed up the debate: "Is the Religious Right Finished?"

As Jerry Falwell pointed out, that question itself is skewed. The "religious right" is the handy terminology of the generally hostile secular media. But aside from the semantics, the question itself suggested that politically active evangelicals need to justify themselves in view of the mounting attitude that the Right had taken a wrong turn.

Reverend Falwell is often targeted as proof of this hypothesis, because he disbanded the Moral Majority in 1989. However, he did so for reasons that actually prove the vitality of evangelical activism. By 1989 there were several national Christian-based organizations that had risen to carry on, and take over the torch lit by Falwell's group.

The title of Jerry Falwell's response in *Christianity Today* sums it up: "I'd Do It All Again." He asks:

> If Christians do not also lead the battle in defense of the unborn, who will? If believers do not oppose same-sex marriages, who will? If people of faith do not aggressively defend religious freedom in the public square, including our public schools, who will? If Christians do not cry out against wickedness in high places, who will? [6]

There are three great challenges we have as we leave the twentieth century. The first is organizational. What will happen as these national leaders prepare to surrender the reins of leadership to the next generation? Will Christians continue to give up the resources of time, talent, and tithe to these groups to enable them to continue to influence the national trajectory of our ship of state? And will these organizations be flexible and innovative enough to meet the ever-changing terrain of the moral battlefields in the coming decades?

The second challenge is individual. It is not about what happens in the offices of a Washington, D.C. organization. It is about what Mrs. Joan Doe Christian in Topeka, Kansas does when her child is handed a condom at public school. It is about what Mr. John Doe Christian in Milwaukee, Wisconsin, does with one night a week: whether he will join a bowling team, or whether he will help a crisis pregnancy center; whether he will use his exhaustion after work as an excuse for noncommitment to civic issues, or whether he will attend a school board meeting to find out why they selected a curriculum that turns traditional moral thinking upside down. The question is not, Why don't "they" do something about our disintegrating nation? The question is, What am I going to do about it?

But all this is "sound and fury signifying nothing," as the Bard says, unless we meet the third challenge. We must see revival in the house of God—and in the houses of God's families—and in the hearts of God's people. When we look at the history of Israel in the Old Testament, there seems to be very little middle ground. God's people were either experiencing the fires of revival, kindled by the fire of the Holy Spirit, and redirected by a shattering collision with the power of God's Word—or else they were led into captivity, and labored under the heavy hand of judgment. Most of us want something in between. A little revival please, but not too much. Nothing fanatical. And certainly none of that judgment business, thank you very much. Not too hot—yet not too cold. Of course, that would then make us lukewarm. The book of Revelation gives us the awful word picture of Jesus spitting the church at Laodicea out of his mouth because they were lukewarm. May that not be us. May we be revived, O Lord. For if we are not, can the twenty-first century hold anything but judgment?

11 Rescuing Victory from the Jaws of Myopia

ONE OF THE arguments of our dissenting brethren, Cal Thomas and Ed Dobson, is that the religious right has not sufficiently proven its efficacy. In other words, our win-loss record does not justify the time, energy, and money (they particularly emphasize, money) invested in large national organizations that have waged battle after battle in America's culture wars. They boldly declare that, regarding abortion, "In perhaps the biggest and costliest battle waged by conservative Christians, twenty years of fighting has won nothing. And our record is no better with other moral and social issues."[1]

However, it has always seemed to us (and we made this point in a live roundtable discussion with them on *Janet Parshall's America*) that by making this argument they are really performing a kind of logician's magic trick. Like any magic trick, their position falls apart when you look closely, and you know what you are looking for.

The main thrust of their argument for a reappraisal of evangelical cultural and political engagement is that the main business of the Church is not temporal but spiritual—the evangelization of souls, not the morals and public welfare of society. While Cal Thomas and Ed Dobson might qualify this slightly (and they do somewhat in their book) to add that there is nothing wrong with voting, peaceful picketing, boycotting, and the like; nevertheless, they believe such things are not the real emphasis of our work as followers of Jesus.

Thus, what they are saying is that political, social, and cultural battles are misguided in their *very first* steps. This means that even if such large-scale crusades turn out to be 100-percent effective in accomplishing their stated political, social, and cultural goals (e.g., banning pornography, returning prayer to public schools, banning abortion), they would have been wrong-headed crusades *by their very definition.* Cal Thomas notes:

> The way in which culture is changed is not by adopting new versions of a strategy that has not worked and cannot work. (If it could, we wouldn't need God, because we could do it all in our own strength.) The way a culture is reclaimed is through people living by different values. The challenge of those who claim to be followers of Jesus Christ is, first and foremost, to be visible evidence of the invisible kingdom of God in our midst. It is to act and think like the One we claim to follow. Did Jesus appeal to Caesar for power or favor?[2]

Yet when Cal Thomas argues that "the change that we seek is more deeply rooted than the legislative process,"[3] that makes the question of whether evangelical social involvement has been "successful" enough a moot issue. In fact, the logical extension of their argument is that achieving victory would actually create more problems for the Church, not fewer. Greater victories would, after all, simply encourage what Thomas and Dobson perceive to be a dangerous trade that we have made: that evangelicals and fundamentalists already "are in danger of substituting our spiritual authority . . . for political authority."[4] If Christians have been wrong in over-emphasizing social and cultural battles because that overemphasis is inconsistent with the mission given to us by Jesus Christ, then that position, if correct, must trump all other questions. All other points, for the Bible-believing Christian, become meaningless. We must, after all, do the bidding of our Lord and Savior, regardless of all "victories" or "defeats" in the worldly sense.

What Thomas and Dobson have done, then, is to use the scorecard of political victories which they themselves would reject as unbiblical, in order to flunk the religious right because it did not sufficiently score enough worldly victories. In defense of this they could indicate that they are simply using the same scorecard for the religious right that those in the Right have followed themselves. But in so doing, they would have assumed that the primary claim-to-fame of the religious right was to achieve the kind of victories that can be tallied on the floor of Congress or in the voting booth.

Such an assumption would be wrong for several reasons. First, while conservative evangelicals certainly have engaged the American culture, hoping to "win" particular battles rather than "lose" them, the motivation for involvement, for most of us, goes far beyond that. We are more interested in being faithful to take a stand for God's eternal principles than in securing temporal victories.

Second, those of us who have been involved in Christian activism know that there is a powerful spiritual, moral, and pedagogical impact when we speak out on the great issues of the day from a Bible-based starting point. Standing for the truth-claim that life is sacred because God created it is a verity in itself. When we act and speak consistently with this truth, we reaffirm, to an increasingly pagan world, the reality of a personal Creator-God. It is a powerful witness to the truth that God exists and that He holds us morally accountable—both individually, and as nations. When we are silent, we deny Him His glory and we deny the essence of who He is. It is impossible to measure the harm to America if, for the last twenty years, the Church had utterly failed to proclaim that pro-life truth. One thing, however, is clear: the loss would be incalculable.

Third, that assumption makes a false choice: we are forced to choose either to adopt a position of being sold-out to a worldly definition of success or to adopt the view that the eternal business of the Church should be our *only* mission statement. But why not a third approach? Why not encourage the Church to make the eternal business of winning souls to Christ its primary business, while at the same time encouraging involvement in the temporal moral issues of the day in a way that is still *consistent* with (and in fact is an *enhancement* of) the winning of souls? While Cal Thomas and Ed Dobson may think this cannot be done, we believe it is not only possible, but it is our clear mandate if we rightly understand authentic evangelism.

There is also a major flaw in the basic *inaccuracy* of the Thomas-Dobson declaration that "twenty years of fighting have won nothing" for involved evangelical Christians. Like so many other questions on this issue, the win-loss ratio cannot be calibrated with clean, mathematical precision. By any standard of measurement, we have won more than we have lost. The gains, both in the particularized sense of individual debates and conflicts, and in the overall position of the Church in America, have exceeded the losses. Stated another way, the rising tide of destruction, moral depravity, and social disintegration in America has been sandbagged, to an impressive degree, by the efforts of the evangelical Church. Thomas and Dobson focus on the icy waters swirling around us, which we are unlikely to prevent. The two of us, rather, focus on the streets and homes that have already been saved from the flood tides.

U.S. Senator Rick Santorum made an interesting observation in a speech at the Heritage Foundation. He noted:

> I believe that we are in a somewhat better place today. A level of access to the public square has been granted to "faith." There is a growing consensus, right and left, that faith has social benefit. Believe in God and you'll live longer. Go to church and you'll stay out of jail. Turn to God and you'll kick your habit. This utilitarian, therapeutic view of faith at least recognizes religion's value to society, and now public policy must recognize it too.[5]

Two practical manifestations of this trend, accordingly to Senator Santorum, are the public positions of two prominent political competitors. He noted that Democratic contender Al Gore had embraced the concept of faith-based organizations helping to solve social problems through "charitable choice." In the same month, Republican front-runner George W. Bush went even further, proposing several ideas to empower faith-based organizations and to encourage them to partner with government and other institutions to help improve America.

Will these positions be consistently held by the candidates? It is impossible to tell. But in our information society there is great value in getting the unified message to the public, from all political parties, that our Churches are an invaluable resource for the public good. This is particularly critical when we consider how, in the last thirty years, the ACLU and other like-minded organizations have attempted to force the cloistering of the Church's message within the walls of the church building, and to keep that message from the streets, marketplaces, and the public squares of our nation.

Perhaps this is an opportune time for the Church to evaluate twenty years of social involvement. If that is the case, then the controversy created by our evangelical brethren will have yielded positive results. A good starting point for such an evaluation is a realistic view of areas where American culture has seen some success at least in part through positions advanced by conservative Christians.

ABORTION

Abortion is in the area where, as the opposing argument goes, our costliest and toughest battle has yielded nothing. In reality, some modest but very important gains have been made.

First and foremost, the rate of abortion is on the decline. While it is impossible to parse the individual impact of pro-life effort on this trend, it must be given some substantial credit. Further, Christians have staffed crisis pregnancy centers around the nation. If you have not visited, supported, or worked in one, there is no better place to see the pro-life philosophy in action. Victories are taking place daily in these humble little centers.

Janet recently gave a speech at a crisis pregnancy center event, and the three-dimensional proof of this pro-life form of activism was impossible to deny. A young couple also addressed the group. Their story was similar to countless others around the country. They had been involved in a "crisis" pregnancy before marriage. They were pressured to abort. Through the work of the local center, they not only saved their baby but they were also introduced to Jesus Christ. As the smiling parents—now born-again Christians and married—held their beautiful baby on the stage, we saw the awesome impact of the whole truth of the whole gospel at work in this wonderful new family.

There has also been a slow but steady solidifying of attitudes among Americans on the pro-life position. In a 1999 poll only 34 percent of Americans felt that *Roe v. Wade* was a change for the better, while 42 percent said the court decision was a change for the worse.[6]

In 1991 a Gallup survey indicated that 49 percent of all Americans considered abortion to be murder. In the intervening nine years since that survey—and considering our saturation from the pro-abortion bias of television, Hollywood, the media, and the implied moral message accompanying the failure to our Courts to reverse the *Roe* decision—one would expect that percentage to have dropped. Instead, that percentage has jumped up by a percentage point, according to a poll taken in 1999. This, coupled with polls indicating that another 28 percent of Americans at least considered abortion to be the taking of a human life, reveal that some 77 percent of all Americans still disapprove of abortion.[7]

In the legal arena, victories have been painstakingly slow and maddeningly incremental in nature. But there have been victories.

In *Hodgson v. Minnesota,* 497 U.S. 417 (1990), the Supreme Court affirmed the right of the state of Minnesota to impose a general requirement of parental notification before a minor child has an abortion. This is a critical area, because pro-abortion public school officials have become brazen in attempting to scurry minors off to abortion clinics without parental input. One such occurrence led to a lawsuit against the Hatboro-Horsham School District in Pennsylvania seeking a court order bringing a halt to such practices. In July 1999 the House of Representatives passed the Child Custody Protection Act. If passed by the Senate and signed by the president, the measure would make it a federal crime to circumvent state parental notification and consent laws by taking minors out of state for abortions.

In *Thornburgh v. American College of Obstetricians and Gynecologists,* 476 U.S. 747 (1986), the Supreme Court permitted some limited areas within which states can regulate abortion and abortion clinics.

In *Planned Parenthood of Southeastern Pennsylvania v. Casey,* 505 U.S. 833 (1992), the Court regrettably refused again to strike down *Roe v. Wade* either in its entirety or in part. But the Court did reverse the reasoning of some of its prior decisions in two areas. First, older cases had suggested a broad prohibition against states requiring the giving of information to mothers intending to abort their babies. This, said the Court in *Casey,* is going too far. The high court ruled that states can require abortionists to disclose "truthful and non-misleading information about the nature of the procedure, the attendant health risks, and those of childbirth, and the 'probable gestational age' of the fetus."[8]

In that same case the Court also overruled prior case law that questioned the constitutionality of a twenty-four-hour waiting period for abortions. Lastly, in *Casey* the Supreme Court ruled that states can not only require parental *notification,* but parental *consent,* as long as procedural guidelines involving judicial bypass are implemented.

We must remember what the pro-abortion folks have been

asking for. They have clamored for absolute abortion on demand—no restrictions, no impediments, and no interference. The Court in *Casey* recognized this. Planned Parenthood was arguing, they noted, that a twenty-four-hour waiting period was "a barrier in the way of abortion on demand." That argument was, in effect, an extension beyond even what *Roe* had expressly held. Thus, to the extent that Planned Parenthood wanted the Court to wander from the gruesomely terrible decision in *Roe* to new lows even farther off the humanity scale, the refusal of the Supreme Court to accommodate them must be seen as a limited victory.

Today more than half of all states have enacted parental involvement laws regarding abortions for minors. Six states have passed laws banning partial-birth abortion. Two more are expected to be added as this book goes to press.[9]

EUTHANASIA

In *Washington v. Glucksberg*, 521 U.S. 702 (1997), the Supreme Court affirmed the right of states to ban physician-assisted suicide. The Court cited studies from the Netherlands, where one survey showed that, as many as one thousand acts of euthanasia were carried out in that country without patient consent, and another almost five thousand lethal doses of morphine were administered without patient consent under their system of doctor-assisted suicide.

In 1999 Maryland became the thirty-eighth state to pass a prohibition against physician-assisted suicide.[10] At long last, Jack Kervorkian is resting comfortably in a jail in Michigan, after numerous unsuccessful attempts by prosecutors to convict him for his acts of "euthanasia" performed in his rusting suicide van.

Religious Freedom

It is difficult to imagine what the state of the law in America would be if groups like the ACLU, Americans United for Separation of Church and State, and People for the American Way had been permitted to roam at will in our court system, unhindered by those sharing our view of freedom.

The American Center for Law and Justice has scored a number of victories in the Supreme Court and lower courts, particularly in cases granting Christian interests the same access to public facilities as other groups. The Rutherford Institute's published reports show it has handled more than 70 percent of all pro-religious freedom, pro-family legal disputes in the nation. Other groups like the Liberty Council, the Pacific Justice Institute, the American Family Law Center, and the Christian Legal Society have provided legal assistance in significant cases involving religious freedom. The Alliance Defense Fund has been created to provide a broad funding mechanism to assist in these kinds of legal battles.

Today when a public school student is told he cannot bring his Bible into the school building, or a Christian group is refused equal access to meeting rooms in a university, or a rescue mission is sued for religious discrimination because it asks homeless folks it feeds to attend a gospel service, there are several Christian-based groups available to help. These scenarios are commonplace to attorneys who handle religious liberty cases. And despite the effort of President Clinton's administration to issue generalized (and toothless) "guidelines" to assist public agencies in handling religious issues, the tide of anti-Christian discrimination has not slowed down.

Our court system is not self-implementing. It requires

attorneys and clients who will stand for truth and freedom and who will engage the opposition and demand that judges do justice. Further, as the old adage goes, justice may be equal, but it is not cheap. It requires money for litigation costs and organizational resources, and it requires the time, sweat, and commitment of men and women who will undergo the intense pressure of courtroom battles that test not only legal issues but moral and personal fiber as well. Those who are resolved to create an entirely secular state and to further censor religious expression have been resisted admirably by our spiritual brethren.

HOMOSEXUAL RIGHTS

The radical homosexual rights movement has steadily applied pressure to secure special civil rights protection in the federal employment field. Thus far, their attempts to amend employment statutes to add sexual orientation as a protected category in employment, on a national basis, have been unsuccessful. Much of the credit belongs not only to the courageous men and women of Congress who resist fierce lobbying from this well-financed and super-organized gay rights contingent, and also from the Christian groups that have encouraged and supported them to vote against such legislation.

Also, efforts to pass "hate crimes" laws, which promote and enhance the image of homosexuals as victims, have also been unsuccessful, due in great measure to the educational efforts of groups like the Family Research Council and Concerned Women for America. In this area in particular, Christians, unless informed of the public policy implications of this kind of legislation, may be lulled into believing that it is harmless—or even beneficial. The passage of such laws would be particularly harmful because if there are hate crimes and hate victims, then we must target and eliminate the haters. But who are the haters? Within hours of the media reports of the beating death of homosexual Matthew Shepard by two men he had met at a bar, America was told who the haters were. Conservative Christians were quickly targeted as responsible for stirring up an atmosphere of hate and, thereby, were somehow vicariously responsible for this senseless murder along a desolate stretch of Wyoming prairie. Never mind, of course, that the two men arrested showed nothing in their background to suggest that they were aligned with the Religious Right, or any other recognizable religious faction, for that matter.

Hate crimes legislation is such a terrible idea, and so destructive to our idea of equality under the law, that prominent New York editor Andrew Sullivan, himself a homosexual, has written persuasively against it. Sullivan argues that "the boundaries between hate and prejudice and between prejudice and opinion and between opinion and truth are so complicated and blurred that any attempt to construct legal and political firewalls is a doomed and illiberal venture."[11] If the Church sleeps this one out, it may wake to find itself having become the official "hate" offender of the twenty-first century.

To the delight of pro-family folks, the Hawaii state Supreme Court finally ruled against the validity of same-sex "marriages" in a lawsuit that had been simmering for some time. Conservative Christian groups had actively opposed the effort by homosexual activists to turn Hawaii into the new "gay Las Vegas" for quick same-sex marriages. Without the ruling same-sex "unions" might have to be recognized as valid by other states under the Full Faith and Credit clause of the U.S. Constitution.

PORNOGRAPHY AND INDECENCY

As part of the Consequences for Juvenile Offenders Act (H.R. 1501), Congress passed a requirement that libraries and schools receiving federal money install Internet filters to screen out child pornography, obscene materials, and other information deemed harmful to minors. The Act also raised the age from sixteen to eighteen regarding the lawful receipt of transported and sold obscene materials.

Congress also passed a resolution calling on Hollywood to implement changes in its portrayal of violence and brutality. While such resolutions are not legally binding, and most have only the slightest symbolic value, this one may be different. Hollywood contributed huge amounts of money through campaign contributions and fund-raisers to keep Bill Clinton in Washington for eight years. Television and movie executives know the importance of political opinions within the beltway of Washington, D.C. After the Littleton, Colorado, shootings and the revelations concerning the shooters' fascination with (and perhaps mimicking of) films like the hyper-violent *The Matrix*, pressure is mounting for some discernible changes in our entertainment culture. It is quite telling that a videotape made by the two boys who did the murdering at Columbine High School shows them debating which Hollywood film director should make the movie of their shooting rampage.

Since the time of the Reagan administration (and its creation of the Attorney General's Commission on Pornography, which included Dr. James Dobson as a member), prosecutions of illegal obscenity and child pornography are now taken seriously by government prosecutors. Numerous committed evangelicals worked in key positions both inside and outside the Justice

Department in an effort to stem the worst of the worst in that corrupt industry. Before we moved to the East Coast, on one of our visits to Washington we dropped in on congressional hearings taking place on the banning of child pornography—and what a sense of victory there was that the issue of child pornography was finally being dealt with.

There is no doubt, that without the changes effected by the conservative–Christian backed Reagan Revolution, the pornography scene would be both unregulated and unimaginable.

WHERE WE GO FROM HERE

This is only a scant review of some of the progress that has been made. But it is also a simple reminder: there is much work to be done, much more territory to claim, and much is at stake. To paraphrase Patrick Henry, exactly when was freedom ever significantly won by a people who chose to recline supinely on their backsides? We need to see the cultural ground that can be won, cultivated, and harvested with the principles of the gospel. And then we need to claim it. It will take God's inspiration. But it will also take our perspiration.

Sam Houston, president of the Republic of Texas, after the battle of San Jacinto, sent a message to General Gaines about his victory. "Tell our friends," he said, "that we have won. Tell them to come on and let the people plant corn." We need to plan beyond "winning" the culture war—we need to tell our friends to get ready to till the ground, to plant and to harvest.

12 The Practical Strategies of Christian Activism

IN THE OLD days, armed conflict was governed by simpler rules—like "don't shoot till you see the whites of their eyes!" Today, in the military as well as in law enforcement agencies like the FBI, things are more sophisticated. Predetermined guidelines regulate anticipated combat, these are referred to as "rules of engagement." The idea is that setting these parameters in advance will help contain and control the field of battle, avoiding unnecessary casualties.

Having been engaged in a variety of skirmishes and battles in the culture war, the two of us are big believers in Christian rules of engagement. The time to formulate these ground rules is not when you are in the thick of the conflict. Instead, these rules need to be worked out in advance—when you can reflect, pray, meditate, and apply the Word of God to your role in impacting your sphere of influence for Christ. Here are the rules we have come to believe are essential when engaging the culture.

1. Learn to listen to the real message of the culture—even where it is wrong.

A common assumption (probably very well-meaning) lurks in

the thinking of evangelicals: that there is something inherently wrong about listening—really listening to what the world is saying about the important matters of God, man, art, politics, ethics, and other great issues. We worry about violating the principle of separation between Christians and the world by taking the things of the world too seriously. We worry about being tainted by carnal interests that are humanistic rather than spiritual.

Missionaries are called to spread the gospel to people of strange cultures and foreign geographies. In order to do that effectively, they must study the cultural practices and language of their target group. They do not study tribal dance so they can enjoy its native aesthetics. They study it to understand how the tribes view the afterlife. If we are to be cultural and spiritual apologists, we must study the culture around us the same way a dedicated missionary studies the lifestyles of a tribal group. The point is to understand what manner of deception has enslaved those whom we are commanded to love into God's kingdom, and to better compare the truth of the gospel to their false worldviews.

Paul's sermon before the Greek philosophers of Athens in Acts 17 is a wonderful example of this principle. First, notice that Paul paid attention to the cultural and religious signposts of Athens when he entered the city. His spirit became provoked when he observed the numerous idols erected on the outskirts of town (v. 16). One of them was dedicated to the "Unknown God." Paul used this prominent memorial as a way to introduce the philosophers to the one true God of whom they were ignorant (v. 23).

Second, Paul was familiar with the Greek poets. As a result, he was able to recite portions of poetry from two famous poets—Epimenides and Aratus—in support of his proofs of the nature of God and His plan to appoint His Son to die and then to be resurrected (vv. 24–31). In order to be effective, our apologetics must be rooted in Scripture; but it must also be knowledgeable about the current moral and spiritual terrain.

Listening to the opposition is the key to any effective defense of our case. Craig learned early as a trial lawyer the sage advice of Abraham Lincoln. The good trial lawyer, Lincoln once quipped, spends 20 percent of his time preparing *his* case and 80 percent of his time preparing his *opponent's* case. Listening to the other side, while not being deceived by the other side, is an important component of being prepared.

Sometimes listening to your opponent also provides an invaluable opportunity to minister to the deep needs of a person who is coming from a position of ignorance about the things of God. Many years ago Janet, as a spokesperson for several pro-life groups, was invited to a series of closed-door meetings with abortion providers and proponents to discuss the pro-life issue. Her first response had been to crumple up the invitation and toss it into the wastepaper basket. *Why go?* she thought. *Surely there can be no compromise on the issue of the sanctity of human life.* But after thinking about it further, she went, burdened in her heart to be a pro-life presence in those discussions while at the same time not flinching on the fundamentals of the pro-life position.

She caught tremendous criticism when the meetings were publicized, particularly when it hit the pages of *People* magazine. Yet in those meetings she learned how even major abortion supporters acknowledge the grief and loss suffered by mothers who abort their babies, and how they acknowledge that the real price of an abortion is the cost of a human life. Janet was able to articulate the reason for her pro-life position in a quiet room, away from the newspaper reporters and the political posturing the issue engenders.

Recently Jerry Falwell was criticized when he met, on the campus of Liberty University, with homosexual leaders to discuss the homosexual rights movement, the need for both sides of the debate to avoid inciting violence, and his Bible-based reasons for preaching that homosexuality is clear and unambiguous sin.

Such meetings would be certainly wrong if they sought to create common moral ground on an issue where the ground can never be common. False peace treaties are sometimes more dangerous than a clearly declared war.

On the other hand, Jesus was never afraid to listen to the arguments of the opposition. What He did—and what we must also do—is to be prepared to answer those unspoken questions lurking in the hearts of the opposition as well to address their public positions.

2. Do your homework.

Much of what is required of the Church gets down to plain old grit, determination, and elbow grease. Most of us would rather change our communities and our nation by one simple, supereffective gesture. We look for a magic potion to rid the nation of abortion, for example. We naively believe that one perfect test case before the Supreme Court, or even the passing of a constitutional amendment banning abortion, will resolve the issue forever. But things are not that easy. Evil is like a malignancy; it needs to be rooted out. But depending on the site, the stage of the cell growth, and the surrounding structures that have been invaded, it very often requires multiple strategies over a long period of time. And it requires persistence.

During the decades-long battle over the outlawing of the

slave trade, William Wilberforce and his antislavery supporters took turns one night a week giving up sleep in order to accomplish the mammoth work needed for the debates in Parliament. We need to count the cost before we get involved in the great moral, spiritual, and cultural battles of the day.

Doing our homework also means being students—all over again. It means, in the realm of public education as an example, reading the trade magazines and scholarly research papers in the education field in order to be able speak the same language and understand the current trends. Much of it will be devastatingly boring. Most will be hard reading. We do not necessarily have to become experts in the field to which we are called. But we do have to be conversant with what the experts in that field have to say, and why they say it.

This requires some rigorous attention to study. One of the problems we have noticed, however, is the tendency of Christians to want to get the *Reader's Digest,* or *Cliffs Notes* versions of the issue—usually a much boiled-down approach garnered from other Christian sources. Beware the tendency to want the Church to tell you what to think about every current issue of the day. Take in what Church leaders have to say, but also know for yourself what God's Word says about it, and then do your own homework!

3. Prepare for the marathon; forget about the short sprint.
Along with the desire for an easy fix for complex problems of our day, evangelicals often feel betrayed and discouraged when what they thought was a quick lap around the track turns into a long-distance run. Craig often jokes about his experience on the high school track team. He was a shot-putter, and at one track meet, a member of the 440-relay team was sick, so they

asked Craig to fill in. Craig had run with the sprinters and distance runners in practice, but he had never done a relay, and certainly not in a meet. From the outside looking in, it was only one lap around the track. But when the starting gun went off, running at the breakneck speed set by the other well-trained athletes, it was a different story. Halfway around the quarter-mile track at full speed, he thought his heart was about to explode and his legs were going to liquefy!

Our son Joseph was a cross-country runner in high school. We watched him jog over hills and valleys, in rain and in sunshine, diligently working to develop strength and endurance. That got us to thinking that this sport in particular truly resembles the current culture wars. The race is long, endurance and pacing are key, and the terrain is rough and rugged. When we prepare and pray for those kind of battles, we should "gird our loins" for the long haul.

4. Don't reinvent the wheel.

In the broad panorama of history, our fellow disciples of Jesus Christ have been working out the balance between the Great Commission and being "salt and light" for two thousand years. If we become students of Church history, we can learn from their mistakes, and we can be encouraged by their accomplishments.

Over the last twenty years, conservative Christians have made a concerted effort to impact culture. A host of organizations, both national and local, have sprung up, applying a Christian worldview to a variety of public policy issues—drug abuse, juvenile delinquency, homosexuality, abortion, family policies, education, religious freedom, national security, pornography, and other public affairs. In the legal arena numerous organizations operate across the nation, seeking to vindicate the rights of

Christians and to protect basic civil liberties from a biblical standpoint. Evangelical groups have been formed to promote Christian worldviews in medicine, nursing, science, the liberal arts, and other academic disciplines.

If we decide to try to make an impact on our local community, we ought to begin by gleaning from the groups that have pioneered the land before us. All of these groups have produced newsletters, research papers, and public information in a variety of forms. If we feel called to a specific kind of Christian activism, we ought to be in contact with such organizations as well as any local cell groups in our area.

5. Act locally but think heavenly.

Liberals have a bit of bumper-sticker philosophy that we would be smart to adopt, with some adjustments. It says: "Act locally but think globally." This recognizes a responsibility to be active in one's local community and immediate sphere of influence. At the same time, that local activism should be in coordination with a broad master plan that has targeted the entire globe for change.

For Christians this philosophy would state: "Act locally but think heavenly." In other words, believers should look for opportunities to impact their local corner of the globe for Christ. First we start in our own "Jerusalem" before impacting "Judea, and Samaria and even to the remotest part of the earth" (Acts 1:8).

At the same time, though, we have to keep God's master plan in mind. This means taking seriously the admonition to "set your mind on the things above, not on the things that are on earth. For you have died and your life is hidden with Christ in God" (Col. 3:2–3). Though we live and work and minister in the world, we are to consider ourselves as if we are "dead" to the earthly desires and motivations of the world (Col. 3:5). Instead, our minds and hearts are renewed by our personal relationship with the Lord Jesus. We think heavenly by permitting Christ to rule in our hearts and minds (Col. 3:10–15).

We are therefore called to bridge two worlds: the earthly one where we stand faithfully for Christ, and God's heavenly kingdom, from which we receive our motivation and which is our ultimate destination.

6. Learn to redefine victory.

The culture wars of the last half of the twentieth century have often involved, at least on the surface, win-or-lose battles. Court decisions, political elections, floor votes in Congress and our state houses over legislation, the votes of our local school board—each of these are measured in the temporal sense by who wins and who loses.

If our local school board votes to distribute contraceptive devices to our children without parental notification, we consider this a defeat for the pro-family forces. When our state legislature passes a law that requires parental notification before a minor gets an abortion, we rightfully claim this to be a victory.

But if we never move beyond this level of win-loss records, we will never understand the ultimate mandate. Janet attended a meeting in the office of a congressman who had consistently voted the "right way"—he had courageously stood up for the principles our nation needs in order to heal itself morally and socially. But he was discouraged. Opposition from others had frustrated almost all of his grand plans for change. This congressman wondered whether those who love the Lord and who want to see right and truth prevail will ever see victory in this current culture. Janet had a wonderful opportunity to encourage him— and to urge him to redefine victory.

When we get to the gates of splendor and our name is called, God will not ask us if we helped pass H.R. 456, or whether we were able to get that last swing vote to restrict abortion, or whether we helped to convince the local city council to take a hard line against the purveyors of pornography. He will be interested in whether we were faithful servants, not if we were successful politicians.

This does not mean that we avoid planning for victory, or that we do not commit ourselves to winning strategies. But it does mean we keep the big picture in mind throughout.

The big picture is to articulate to those within our sphere of influence the objective truth about good and evil, and about those values that build up and those that destroy. Further, whenever possible and wherever appropriate, we should share that the source of our knowledge of objective truth comes from God, who has communicated truth to all of us through His revealed Word. Each defense of the truth, each position for justice, each shared vision from the principles of His Word is a piece of the mosaic. We are not here just to win public policy battles; we are here to point the way to Him in everything we do. Our lives, our positions on public issues, and the *way* in which we fight "the good fight" all paint a picture of who He is for a world that has lost its way.

In pursuing this truth-telling function, we should remember the Old Testament prophets. They were reviled, stoned, and sawed in two. While there are victories like the one in Jonah, where the entire nation-state of Nineveh responded to his preaching, more often the prophets were scorned or killed and their message ignored.

Does that mean that most of them failed? Certainly not. It means that they were faithful to a God who is ever faithful to us.

The prophets were faithful, even when they were unable to see all of the details of God's majestic plan. The involvement of the believing Church in the current cultural collapse is a prophetic one. Like the prophets of old, we are speaking hard truths to those who yearn to have their ears tickled with soft words of groundless optimism. Our primary identification must be as servants of the Most High God. What is the essence of servant-hood? It is faithfulness. Jesus made that point explicitly in Matthew 24. The problem comes in our attitude toward being faithful when the environment around us has become decidedly hostile.

Recently we came across a cartoon in a magazine. It showed a Roman coliseum with bodies littered across the foreground. A lion has a piece of chalk in its hand and is keeping score on a board. It said something like this—"Christians 0, Lions 20."

Christians need to stop asking the lions to tell us what the score is. The only real score is the "well done" we will get from the One who will ultimately make even the lion to lie down with the lamb.

7. Be a bricklayer, not a stone thrower.

One of the sobering things we have discovered is the way in which personal energy is improperly—and sometimes maliciously—misdirected. Too many Christians would rather throw a thousand stones than to lay a single brick.

This is not to say that there is never a time when biblical rebuke or correction is necessary. Nor does it mean that we should become intimidated into silence when we see a ministry in which we hold a position of responsibility heading in an unbiblical direction. But our efforts, and our energies, ought to be positive whenever possible.

When we do that, several things happen. First, taking a positive and productive approach to problem solving (as opposed to cultivating the "spiritual gift" of criticism) is ultimately the most utilitarian strategy. It is amazing to realize how much could be accomplished if we were to channel all that energy of ill will that builds up over things we do not like and apply it in a way that changes things for the better.

More important, spending time in gripe sessions and backbiting is just plain unbiblical. If we have any questions about God's condemnation of murmuring and attitudes of disgruntlement, we should read how He handled it in Numbers 11!

There is important work to be done—giants in the land to be slain: abortion, pornography, divorce, rampant crime, injustice in the courts, loss of religious freedom, assaults on the freedom and integrity of the family, government oppression, mayhem in our public educational system, and drug addiction. This is no time for griping and stewing. This is the time for letting the Creator of the universe use us to create order out of chaos. It is the time to stand for the right, the true, and the good—the time to shine a beacon of light in the midst of a darkened and dismal landscape.

8. Follow the Nehemiah principle.

The Old Testament story of Nehemiah and the rebuilding of the walls of Jerusalem holds multiple lessons for us. They are all incredibly practical. But one of the best is the lesson of keeping first things first, even when external forces are howling around you for attention and threatening to disrupt your focus.

Nehemiah, the royal cupbearer to King Artaxerxes, had a vision of rebuilding the holy city of Jerusalem for the people of God. The city, which had been overrun by the invading pagan armies, had been destroyed and its protective walls leveled. This was no mere personal ambition of Nehemiah; it was something God had put into his mind (Neh. 2:12).

After he explained his heart's burden to the Babylonian king, Nehemiah was granted permission to collect the necessary construction materials and take them to Jerusalem to begin the rebuilding project.

However, opposition arose quickly from the local pagans. First it came in the form of harassing crowds who gathered at the building site to mock the efforts. Accusing Nehemiah's followers of poor workmanship in constructing the wall, they cried out, "If a fox should jump on it, he would break their stone wall down!" (4:3).

Then things turned violent. The enemy conspired to destroy the project through physical attack. When Nehemiah learned of the conspiracy it would have been easy to hunker down into a full-court defense, stopping the work to focus merely on the battle. Instead, he wisely kept his focus on the spiritual mission God had given him, while making pragmatic plans to defend against the attackers. Nehemiah had the construction workers continue building with their tools in one hand and a weapon in the other (4:17). He also formed a strategic plan. He established a prearranged rallying point along the wall in the event of an attack. If the warning trumpet blew, all of the workers would grab their spears and shields and meet at the rallying point for their orders (4:20).

It is critical to anticipate the inevitable attacks when we enter into any controversial arena. It is also critical to have a plan in place to be able to continue the work God has called us to when the assaults start coming in over the walls. Attack may come in the form of public criticism. Expect some nasty letters to the editor of the local newspaper naming you by name. Your friends or neighbors may start distancing themselves from you. There may be hostility against you at the next neighborhood block party or PTA meeting. Folks at your church may even give you some advice "in the Lord" to quit the fight. Colleagues and associates who had previously been friendly and supportive may turn against you.

But if the Lord has truly called you to the task, and if you are doing the task in a godly and biblical fashion so as not to intentionally give offense to anyone, be prepared for the opposition and be committed to keeping your focus on the task.

There is also a temptation to become overly involved and to quickly burn out when it comes to taking a stand for the truth of God in matters of public controversy. The two of us refer to this as starting with the "Aha!" experience. This is the stage where one wakes up to the powerful and disturbing reality of sin and evil at work in the world—when one realizes that there are forces at work, even unwittingly, that threaten to undermine our freedom, our families, and our faith, or threaten to destroy our communities.

Next there is the "Heigh-Ho" phenemenon, where one rallies to some commitment of time, energy, or money (or perhaps all three) to the cause, hoping to make a real difference.

But as one researches the issue and gets involved, suddenly there is that sinking feeling that the problem is more complex than originally imagined. Then there is the realization that there are a host of other problems and issues and evils out there. Being only one person just does not feel sufficient. In fact, it is easy to feel overwhelmed, discouraged, and ultimately defeated. This is the "Oh No" experience.

One of the things we have learned, sometimes the hard way, is to keep our focus on those things we feel God has called us to.

As for the other battles, we will offer our prayer support and will consider giving our tithe—but we will decline spreading ourselves too thin. If you are just starting to get involved in taking the truth of the gospel out into the cultural battles of your community, start slowly and stick to a single task and a single issue at first, in an area where the Lord has touched your heart. After all, you serve the same Lord Jesus who miraculously multiplied a handful of bread and fish to feed thousands. Surely He can take your modest efforts and multiply your effectiveness several times over.

9. Pray for the other side.

Nothing will get our perspective right quicker and more effectively than to start praying for those who oppose what we believe—even those who oppose and persecute us, even those who have harmed us, our family, or friends.

Stephen, the first-century Christian martyr, was a powerful example of this. He gave a breathtaking and indicting sermon to an angry mob, convicting them to the marrow of their bones for their rejection of Jesus Christ as the Messiah. The book of Acts records that the mob became so enraged at his words that "they began gnashing their teeth at him" (7:54).

But Stephen was "full of the Holy Spirit" (7:55). As they stoned him to death his last words before entering glory were, "Lord, do not hold this sin against them" (7:60). These words were similar to those of Jesus, who, while dying a cruel execution, prayed for His enemies (Luke 23:34).

Praying for those who oppose us not only solicits the supernatural power of God to change the hearts of the other person, it also softens our own hearts in the process. This heart-softening process is, in turn, integral to the last of our rules of engagement.

10. Speak the truth in love.

A number of years ago, Craig was scheduled to give a speech in Minnesota. We traveled together to the Minneapolis area for the event. While there we saw an article from a local newspaper about an incident that occurred in a tiny town in Minnesota. The pastor of a small country church had made some public comments criticizing a recent AIDS curriculum the school board was considering. As a result, the homosexual community came out swinging. When the pastor was finishing his Sunday service in his little country church, a huge group of lesbian and homosexual activists arrived on motorcycles. They formed a circle around the church, and as the members and their families began exiting through the front doors, the motorcyclists began screaming insults at them, harassing and threatening them. While this incident was unusual and disturbing, it is not isolated. Radical groups like ACT UP are notorious for disrupting church services in an effort to get their point across.

But what about Christian engagement on those same issues? We remember another incident in a metropolitan area involving a volatile battle over homosexual issues in a public school curriculum. The school board meeting was expected to draw such large crowds that it was moved from the boardroom into an auditorium. Conservative Christians were there by the hundreds. Three homosexual activists were sitting quietly in the front row of the auditorium, holding signs. We had come to know them personally through several media debates the two of us had been involved in with them.

While they sat in the auditorium waiting for the meeting to start, the three activists were surrounded by about a dozen opponents who shouted at them angrily. The mood quickly became very ugly. The shouting and name calling against the homosexuals by those on "our side" of the debate continued until the chairman gaveled the meeting to order. During a break in the meeting, we approached the three of them and apologized for the conduct of the group that had berated and intimidated them.

If Christians are going to be successful in these cultural and spiritual battles, especially the volatile ones, we have to learn to separate the *sinner* from the *sin*—to separate the *public policy* issue from the *person*. The ultimate aim is not just to win the important case, or to oppose bad policy, or to pass good legislation. The ultimate goal is to love the other side to the cross of Christ while convicting them with the truth.

It is not a multiple-choice test for the followers of the Lord Jesus Christ, who have been called to be His ambassadors. We do not have the choice of either *love* or *truth*. We are commanded to exercise *both*. The watching world expects to see us seethe with hate and condemnation, to strut in self-righteousness. This is the distorted picture that has been painted of us. We must explode that myth and show the love and humility that come from knowing that "there is therefore now no condemnation for those who are in Christ Jesus" (Rom 8:1). Because as we have escaped condemnation by God's grace through faith in Christ, we need to show mercy on those who are still entrapped by the lies of the enemy.

13 | The Christian and the Courts

PEOPLE NOT INVOLVED in law-related fields sometimes get the impression that while court battles may be occasionally interesting or entertaining, they are rather remote, confusing, and irrelevant. Furthermore, nonlawyers may get the feeling that there is little they can do to effect change in the courts—particularly in the seemingly impregnable and lofty chambers of the Supreme Court. That is where they are wrong.

One of the most powerful tools at the disposal of any president—an official that we elect with our votes—is his power to nominate judges to sit on the Supreme Court. Of course, a majority of the Senate is required to confirm the nominations. But then again, the members of the Senate are also elected by the American public. So all of us, in the election of our president and U.S. senators, end up having a weighty role in that process. It is likely that our next president will have at least one—and perhaps even several—opportunities to exercise that awesome responsibility.

One such judicial nomination in 1937 had repercussions on the issue of our religious liberties that are still being felt today.

THE NEW BERLIN WALL

On August 12, 1937, President Franklin D. Roosevelt nominated Hugo Black to the Supreme Court. Black had been an Alabama lawyer before the First World War. He joined the army, and after the war went into politics. Black ran successfully for the U.S. Senate in 1926 and was reelected in 1932. He had never been a judge.

Some historians believe that by nominating the extremely liberal Hugo Black, President Roosevelt was getting his ultimate revenge on the conservative members of the Senate who had managed to thwart FDR's coveted reorganization bill. The reaction in the Senate when they heard who was being nominated is described this way:

> The resultant silence was stupendous. The conservative Democrats and Republicans could not have been more horrified to learn that Satan himself had been appointed to the High Court . . . The stunned victors of the Court fight slowly realized that FDR was having his revenge.[1]

While it must be noted that Hugo Black did not, single-handedly, redirect the interpretation of church-state relations on the Court, nevertheless he was a vocal supporter of an extreme separation of the two.

In 1947 Hugo Black wrote the opinion for the majority in the case of *Everson v. Board of Education,* which dealt with a constitutional challenge to state-supported transportation for parochial school children. The case required the Court to interpret the religion clause of the First Amendment, which deals with the relationship between government and religion: "Congress shall make no law respecting an establishment of religion, or prohibiting the free exercise thereof."

The first clause ("respecting an establishment of religion") is commonly referred to as the *establishment clause*, and it limits government's ability to "establish" (to officially promote or impose on others) a religious position. The second clause ("or prohibiting the free exercise thereof") is the *free exercise clause*. It offers a bulwark of protection for religious believers against the oppressive actions of government. It is clear that the founding fathers and drafters of the Constitution had a broad and expansive view of individual religious liberties. The question in *Everson* was whether, 150 years later, our nation's highest court would remember that.

In its precise result, the *Everson* case was unremarkable. The court concluded that public provision of busing transportation for students in private religious schools did not violate the First Amendment's prohibition on establishment of religion.

But Justice Black authored a majority opinion that contained language so hostile to the idea of any working relationship between religion and government that the reasoning he used seems wholly at odds with the actual holding of the case.

Underlying the Supreme Court's misunderstanding of the dynamic between church and state was the counterfeit jurisprudential currency adopted in Black's opinion, which used the concept of a "wall of separation between church and state." That now famous phrase, minted by the Court in that 1947 decision, came almost entirely from one source—a letter written by Thomas Jefferson in 1802 to the Danbury Baptist Association. Jefferson had used the phrase as a reference to general ideals of religious freedom, as indicated by his concern, in that letter, with the "rights of conscience." He considered the liberty of religious conscience to be among our "natural rights." Jefferson was interested in avoiding only the exercise of the official establishments of national religion; he was keenly concerned with individual rights of religion. In the *Everson* case, however, the Supreme Court used the "wall of separation" language as a sword against *any* commingling between government and religion.

Black's decision in the *Everson* case described the wall of separation between church and state as "high and impregnable," which could not afford even the "slightest breach."[2] His opinion recited a long list of things that *could not* be done between the religious sphere and the public sphere. For the first 150 years of our national life, America had lived without this wall of separation. Now, in 1947, the Supreme Court painted that concept into the language of the First Amendment with broad, breathtaking strokes.

It is important to measure the great distance the Supreme Court had leapfrogged, in one single decision in 1947, from the original understanding of the Founders, who favored religious accommodation, to this newly constructed "high and impregnable wall." When the original language of the First Amendment was being debated and refined on the floor of Congress in 1789, James Madison was the primary draftsman. Significantly, one of Madison's earlier drafts of the "religion clauses" emphasized that the intent to prohibit the establishment of a national religion, not create an impregnable wall between religious faith and the public sphere. On June 8 of that year, during debate on the Amendments, Madison introduced the following language for approval by Congress: "The civil rights of none shall be abridged on account of religious belief or worship, nor shall any *national religion* be *established,* nor shall the full and equal rights of conscience be in any manner, nor on any pretext infringed."[3]

Unfortunately for posterity, Madison was forced to deal with the political realities of those who had feared, and opposed, the creation of a federal Constitution. The Anti-Federalists were suspicious of any constitutional language that might even indirectly permit the creation of a strong, centralized national government that would undermine state sovereignty. In order to appease that group, Madison grudgingly withdrew his proposal, which had made reference to avoiding the establishment of a "national religion"—not because of any disagreement as to the limits of state-church relations, but because he needed the votes of those who feared any use of the word *national*. Shortly afterward, Madison, in collaboration with others, proposed the language that is our current version of the First Amendment.

This sequence of events is instructive. It tells us that the chief draftsman of the First Amendment believed that the only area of church-state interaction that should be constitutionally banned as an illegal "establishment" was the creation of a national religion. That concern is a far cry from the long parade of public activities that the Supreme Court would begin striking down after 1947.

One year after the *Everson* decision, the church-state separation doctrine was again wielded by the high Court, this time to strike down activities that were carried on within the public schools. In *McCollum v. Board of Education*, in an opinion again authored by Justice Black, the Court banned the practice of public schools inviting community religious leaders to provide *voluntary and optional* discussion on religious topics—even if no public money went to the project, and even if it was supported totally by private contributions. There was an immediate protest from religious leaders. The Catholic Bishops of the United States decried the decision as a "judicial establishment of secularism." Under the strict reasoning of *McCollum*, no public school could have a guest lecture by a rabbi on the cultural history of Hanukkah, or by a pastor on the Christmas nativity story, or by a Muslim about Ramadan, even if it coincided with a course on the cultural diversity of America.

PRAYER AND BIBLE READING: THE NEW CONTAGION

In order to see how this wall of separation really began to affect American society, we need to bring our camera lens down very close to the contours and topography of a decision of the U.S. Supreme Court in 1962: the case of *Engel v. Vitale*. Stated simply, that decision was wrong about prayer and public schools. In fact, the Court in the *Engel* case, more than any other decision, officially rendered God *persona non grata* (an unwelcome person) in the public schools of our nation. While the precise result of the case is not entirely objectionable (few of us care for teacher-led prayers in public school), the reasoning it employed paved the way for a bitter harvest of court decisions we are still reaping today.

The case concerns the use of a short, nondenominational, voluntary prayer (known as the "Regent's Prayer") at the beginning of the school day in the public schools of the state of New York. Under the interpretation of the lower courts, student participation was purely *voluntary,* and schools were required to exempt from these activities the children of any objecting families, so they would be free from any "embarrassments and pressures."

As a side note, there are thousands of religious families in America today who would covet the same consideration, regarding the right to exempt their children from instruction that defiles their religion or violates their beliefs, that dissenting families were provided in New York regarding the right not to hear a thirty-second prayer.

On June 25, 1962, however, a five-justice majority of the Supreme Court ruled in the *Engel* case that, voluntary or not, these prayer activities were illegal because they violated the establishment clause of the First Amendment. Throughout the decision, the Court addressed the supposed dangers of government-composed prayers. Now, in truth, we do see public policy problems with school-composed prayers led by school officials; but that was not the question addressed by the Supreme Court. They were dealing with the issue of whether voluntary prayer activities in public school violated the establishment clause. Viewing the First Amendment in the context of the original understanding of its framers, such prayers, if truly voluntary, should not have been held to violate the Constitution. And as to the *voluntary* prayers by students *on their own initiative*, or by *private citizens*, in any setting (including the schools), there is almost nothing in the history surrounding the creation of the establishment clause that would justify outlawing those kind of activities.

To the contrary, with only a miniscule number of exceptions, our highest public officials who were present at the formation of the Constitution and the later ratification of the Amendments actively and regularly engaged in public prayers and proclamations asking for God's blessings and guidance on our nation.

In *Engel*, the Court headed by Hugo Black, made the astounding (and incorrect) statement that "It is a matter of history that this very practice of establishing government composed prayer for religious services" was one of the reasons for early colonists to leave England for the religious freedom of the colonies. No credible view of history would support this. David Ramsey, considered one of the greatest early American historians, wrote in *The History of the American Revolution*, published in 1789, that the early settlers and Puritans came out of both a dread of arbitrary government power and the desire to secure religious freedom, among other things. But they did not fear, let alone really care about, the fact that England was composing official prayers—what they feared were official acts imposing certain forms of required church worship and prohibiting others. At the very epicenter of the intent behind the religion clauses of the First Amendment was a concern, not with the right to be free from the presence of religion, but the freedom from being compelled to practice or profess a religion at odds with personal conscience.

To make matters worse, the Court in *Engel* failed to cite even one Supreme Court decision, or one court case of any kind, to support its conclusion. This embarrassing fact was admitted by the Court in the 1963 decision in the *Abington School District* case, which banned Bible reading and the Lord's Prayer from public schools. However, the Court excused the total absence of citation to any precedent in *Engel* on the grounds that its decision in that case had been based on "principles . . . (which were) universally recognized."[4] While there are such things as self-evident truths (some of them are listed in the Declaration of Independence—most notably that our liberties come from our divine Creator), it would not appear that banning prayer from public school qualifies as one of them.

But perhaps the ultimate *coup de grace* was the Court's conclusion in the *Engel* case that its decision agreed with the intent of the Founding Fathers. Nothing could be farther from the truth.

Thomas Jefferson had repeatedly emphasized that the real threat to religious liberty was the specter of government using its power to impose religion on citizens or to compel them against their consciences—using the coercion of the state by punishment or loss of civil rights to enforce the state's dictates on religion. Jefferson said as much in his authorship of the preamble to The Statute of Virginia for Religious Freedom, drafted in 1777 and adopted in 1786. Jefferson, a founder of the University of Virginia, permitted and endorsed the use of prayer and invocation at the first recorded graduation ceremonies there.

James Madison, during the debates on the Bill of Rights, said that the religion clause of the First Amendment was concerned with the freedom from being compelled to worship in any way contrary to the dictates of conscience. As president, in 1813, 1814, and again in 1815, he issued official proclamations for national prayer and thanksgiving to God. There are countless examples of other founders, like John Adams, who expressed similar public accommodation to prayer and religious practice in their writings and official governmental acts.

A dissenter in the *Engel* case, Justice Potter Stewart, predicted that such decisions would cause, not the "realization of state neutrality, but rather . . . the establishment of a religion of secularism" if carried to their logical extreme.[5] We believe Justice Stewart was absolutely correct.

With only a few exceptions, this stilted concept of the separation of church and state has dominated the decisions of the Supreme Court and the lower federal courts for half a century. There is a growing consensus that the Court is not likely to repent of its error any time soon, and that it is time to settle the matter through an amendment to the Constitution.

But whether cured by constitutional amendment or otherwise, the prayers of students and other private persons in public settings must *not* be treated as a kind of constitutional contagion, as if it had to be quarantined for the public benefit. That kind of approach violates the principles of equality that Madison declared to be the very basis of all law. Religious speech, including prayer, has been treated like the illegitimate offspring of free speech—not just a second-class citizen, but an illegal alien in the constitutional landscape where almost all other forms of expression (as long as they are not religious) are protected.

PARADE OF CHURCH-STATE HORRIBLES

In the three decades since the *Engel* and *Abington School District* cases, the Supreme Court has continued to issue rulings that have added more bricks to the "Berlin Wall" of separation.

In 1980 the High Court again confronted the role of religion in public schools. The case was *Stone v. Graham.* The Kentucky Supreme Court had ruled that a state law that required the posting of the Ten Commandments in every public school building was constitutional. However, the United States Supreme Court reversed the Kentucky court decision and ruled that it was a violation of the establishment clause of the First Amendment. This was so, the court said, even though the Ten Commandments plaques in question contained explicit statements disclaiming any religious endorsement. The disclaimer confirmed that the displays were merely a reminder of how those ancient and almost universally accepted moral rules had contributed to our Western idea of law.

The true irony is that within the Supreme Court chamber itself is a mural depicting Moses with the Ten Commandments. The result in the case, which banned the display of that moral code from public schools, seemed to be an embarrassing anomaly when contrasted with the religious symbolism on the walls of the Court. It was not long before a lower federal court, following suit, banned the display of the Ten Commandments from the walls of court buildings.

Five years later the Supreme Court revisited the religion–public school debate, this time dealing with an Alabama law that provided for school days to begin with a moment of silence or prayer. The fact that prayer was an option was enough for the Supreme Court to strike down the provision as a violation of the establishment clause in *Wallace v. Jaffree*. Justice Rehnquist, in a dissenting opinion, chastised the majority of the Court for relying on the "faulty" wall of separation concept. He described that phrase as "a metaphor based on bad history, a metaphor which has proved useless as a guide to judging," concluding that "It should be frankly and explicitly abandoned." Unfortunately, the majority of other justices have refused his invitation.

In 1987 the ACLU brought a lawsuit challenging Louisiana's "balanced treatment" law a legislative attempt to insure that evolution would not be given a monopoly over the marketplace of ideas in public school classrooms. The law provided that the teaching of evolution should be counterbalanced with the offering of other explanations about the theory of origins—like creationism. For the majority of the Supreme Court, however, such alternative explanations for the origin of the universe, if they are not evolutionary, *must* not be *scientific*. And if such explanations are not scientific, then they must be *religious*. The Court struck down the law because it concluded that its "preeminent purpose . . . [was to] clearly advance the religious viewpoint that a supernatural being created humankind." The upshot of that case, *Edwards v. Aguillard*, was to permit the theory of evolution to secure a lock-grip monopoly in the world of ideas in every public school in the nation.

Two years later the ACLU argued another church-state separation case before the Supreme Court. At issue was the legality of a Christmas nativity display that had been placed in the foyer of a public building in Pittsburgh. This time the legal arguments presented by the lawyers mirrored an internal dispute within the Court itself. During the Christmas holiday of the very session when the Court would hear argument in *County of Allegheny v. American Civil Liberties Union,* a group of law clerks to the more liberal justices filed a protest with Chief Justice William Rehnquist regarding the usual seasonal activities of the Court.

The tradition of the Court included displaying a huge Christmas tree in the foyer of the Supreme Court building and singing Christmas carols. In the past Justice Thurgood Marshall had refused to participate in such activities on the grounds that he "still believ[ed] in the separation of church and state." Now a number of the law clerks of the Court were following suit. Chief Justice Rehnquist met with several of them but refused to discontinue the holiday festivities.[6]

Unfortunately, the nativity scene in Pittsburgh that was involved in the *County of Allegheny* case met with a more heavy-handed fate. A deeply divided Court ruled that the traditional crèche was too overtly religious and placed too conspicuously in a public building to pass constitutional muster. That decision was another warning shot fired into the night sky. The American public was being warned that almost any religious symbol or activity, displayed in public, was constitutionally suspicious.

Not all courts have followed the separate opinions of the splintered majority of justices in the *Allegheny* decision to its logical conclusion. Several years after that case, Craig argued a similar case before the Wisconsin Supreme Court. It involved a lawsuit brought by the Freedom from Religion Foundation in an effort to ban a Christmas nativity scene erected by village officials just outside Madison, the state capital. The attorney for the Foundation, a former Attorney General of Wisconsin, argued that the traditional crèche lacked the sufficient *secularizing* elements (plastic reindeer, striped candy canes, glowing Santa, etc.). As a result, they claimed the display was too religious and therefore violated the separation of church and state. The display honoring the birth of Christ was in a prominent village park, was lighted, and was only accompanied by a Christmas tree and a sign celebrating the freedom of religion.

Craig argued the case for the village officials. He had not been in the courtroom of that state supreme court for a while. When the little green light on the attorney's podium turned on, signaling the beginning of the allotted time for him to present his oral argument, he walked up to the podium and then glanced up at the ornate painted murals that surrounded the high walls of the courtroom. Several scenes depicted events of religious importance from history, including the prominent inclusion of the Christian cross. How fruitless, he commented to the Justices, is any attempt to avoid the reality of spiritual values or to try to deny the validity and appropriateness of religious symbolism in the American experience, as the murals of the courtroom so aptly illustrated.

The Wisconsin Supreme Court ruled that the display did not violate either the U.S. Constitution or the Wisconsin Constitution, noting the conflicting and uncertain nature of the U.S. Supreme Court's decisions on the issue. The Wisconsin court held that the mere *recognition* by cities and villages of the Christian origins of our holidays or other aspects of our cultural heritage is constitutional and does not rise to an illegal *endorsement* of Christianity as an official state religion. Unfortunately, not all courts exercise that kind of wisdom when it comes to the presence of religion in the public square.

The U.S. Supreme Court has continued to issue decisions that treat the issue of religious expression with little accommodation, and occasionally with overt hostility. Recently the Court ruled on the Religious Freedom Restoration Act (RFRA), which had been passed by Congress in an attempt to more adequately protect the free exercise of religion. The Court struck down that federal law as an improper exercise of congressional authority. The clear implication of the decision was that the Supreme Court considers itself, and itself alone, as the sole branch of government permitted to interpret the nature and breadth of our religious liberties. That fact would not be so troublesome except that they have reduced those liberties with nearly every succeeding decision.

The only way around this dilemma is to enact an amendment to the Constitution that will restore the First Amendment to the vision of the founders. An attempt at this came in the 105th Congress, with the Religious Freedom Amendment (House Joint Resolution 78). Craig had the opportunity to work with Congressman Ernest Istook and other key members of Congress and conservative groups in drafting and promoting the RFA. However, though history was made by its being voted upon on the House floor, it gained only a majority of votes, not enough for the two-thirds needed for passage.

The RFA has been introduced again, but its success will depend on the political composition of Congress. And the composition of Congress will depend, in great measure, on the willingness of the Church to engage our political process.

Jonathan Maxcy, an early American preacher and later president of four prestigious colleges, said it this way: "No government except absolute despotism, can support itself over a people destitute of religion . . . the American people, therefore, have no way to secure their liberty but by securing their religion."[7] Issues of religious liberty are first principles upon which all our other freedoms depend.

THE ONCE AND FUTURE COURT

When Supreme Court justices come to these kinds of broad questions of church-state relations, it is impossible for them to ignore their own presuppositions and worldview. Justice Byron White once noted that when justices choose a constitutionally uncharted course of action in jurisprudence, they necessarily "carve out what they deemed to be the most desirable national policy."[8] And in a revealing bit of candor, Justice Robert Jackson noted that in trying to determine what is "secular" and what is "sectarian" in terms of the separation of church and state, the justices invariably "find no law but their own presuppositions."[9]

While we have focused on religious liberty in this chapter, what we have said about the evolving (and troubling) state of the law could also be said about abortion and other issues.

Given that the underlying presuppositions of our justices inevitably play a part in decisions of tremendous constitutional importance, it becomes paramount that we elect officials who will pick the right future members of the Supreme Court. Since Bill Clinton's election as president, he has been able to place two justices on the Supreme Court: Ruth Bader Ginsburg, and Stephen Breyer. Both justices have consistently cast votes in church-state cases that place more (not fewer) bricks on the "Berlin Wall of separation" between church and state. Both have manifested a position of relative hostility to the idea of expanding freedom of religious expression.

An ad placed in the November 12, 1999, *New York Times* spells out what is at stake if pro-life, pro-family, pro-religious liberty Christians withdraw from the public debate. The ad was sponsored in part by the Religious Coalition and Catholics for a Free Choice. A portion of it read:

AN ABORTION IS EVERY WOMAN'S RIGHT
In the year 2000,
two justices will be
76 years old or older
WOMEN MUST HAVE A PRO-CHOICE PRESIDENT

Great issues involving the sanctity of human life and the future of religious freedom hang in the balance in our nation. Those who would radically redefine and obliterate these paramount interests have no intention of retreating, as this advertisement clearly shows. The question becomes, What are you—what are we—committed to doing in our lifetimes to reverse the direction of our courts? Christian lawyers need to help direct the judicial decision-making process in our nation. But even more important, Christian citizens need to use the profound stewardship of democracy to hold our leaders and our judicial system accountable. If we do, then we may yet realize those enduring principles of Amos 5:15: "Hate evil, love good, and establish justice in the gate!"

14 | The Republican Party: A Not-So-Modern Morality Tale

IF WE ARE to be good students of the culture, and therefore effective Christian apologists, we need to strip back the labels the mainstream media tosses to us and go to the deeper truths. Often Christians dismiss what is being debated, particularly during an election year, as mere "politics as usual." If we take that *laissez-faire* attitude, particularly when Christians are being painted unfairly into a corner and portrayed as extremists, we will lose the big picture in terms of where mainstream culture is today.

CHRISTIAN CONSERVATIVES AS PUNCHING BAGS

Take, for example, the battle for the Republican primaries in 1999–2000. From New Hampshire on, presidential candidate John McCain was knighted by the press. At one point, McCain's face appeared on the covers of *Time, Newsweek,* and the *Weekly Standard*—all in the same week.

At the same time, the media zeroed in on the George W. Bush campaign like a great white shark in a feeding frenzy. First, Mr. Bush was criticized for having addressed the students at Bob

Jones University, a private Christian fundamentalist college in South Carolina. Every talk show program was discussing whether George W. Bush had lost his moral authority to lead because he appeared on a campus that still had on its books a rule against interracial dating. Further, McCain implied that Bush must have an anti-Catholic bias if he appeared on the campus of a fundamentalist school. Ignored, of course, was the fact that candidates Ronald Reagan and Bob Dole had also made campaign stops at this same college when they were running for president; their visits had caused nary a ripple.

The whole issue died when Bob Jones III, president of Bob Jones University, appeared on *Larry King Live!* and announced that the university would abolish its rule on interracial dating. Before the matter disappeared off the public radar screen, however, Democrats in Congress called for an official resolution condemning Bob Jones University. Apparently, no one on Capitol Hill in favor of that resolution considered the clear implications of such a move: it was nothing short of anti-Christian bigotry by federally elected officials.

Next, John McCain went after George W. Bush over what he perceived were Bush's ties to the Christian right. Again, the national media aired McCain's tirade against Pat Robertson and Jerry Falwell, whom he portrayed as part of the "forces of evil" (a comment later dismissed by McCain as a failed attempt at humor), "reprehensible," and "agents of intolerance."[1] Later, when McCain appeared on *Hardball,* he refused to retract his comments, indicating that they had been "carefully thought out."[2]

Not to be outdone, Al Gore then took potshots at Bush, commenting about a supposed secret meeting between George W. Bush, Jerry Falwell, and Pat Robertson. Gore's ploy was to try to paint Bush as a Christian extremist who had already made deals with evangelical leaders over future Supreme Court nominations.

The national press did little to clear the air of these bigoted attacks and unfounded charges. Janet invited Jerry Falwell on *Janet Parshall's America* on March 6, 2000 to get the rest of the story. Here is what unfolded.

Parshall   My heart has been hurting just hearing how much you have been demonized in the last few days. Were you surprised at this? Did you see this coming?

Falwell   I really did not. I thought Senator McCain would be too wise to make such a terrible mistake. I've always been an admirer of Senator McCain. On *This Week with Sam Donaldson and Cokie Roberts* yesterday, I made the statement that, if he were to win the nomination, he would certainly have my vote—although we would have some differences—but I would sure prefer him over Al Gore. Anyone who spent five years in a communist prison camp—for me and all Americans—is worthy of my adoration. But, at the same time, the things that he said . . .

I've never said—nor do I believe—that the president is a murderer. He's a moral reprobate, but I don't think for a moment that he's ever taken anybody's life, nor have I said it or intimated it. I think the senator knows that.

Parshall   Let me ask you what you think he means. A lot of Americans who have a very passive interest in

American politics might be questioning, "What does he mean when he talks about your being exclusionary?" In fact, again and again and again, the mantra John McCain quotes is that he wants to be the party of addition, not the party of division. Why would he marginalize you, thereby being divisive?

Falwell I haven't the foggiest idea. He and I have never met; I've never had a letter from him. I have to look at it totally as a political ploy. Some young kids around his campaign thought, *If we hit the Christians—if we attack the leaders of the conservative Christians in the country—maybe we can turn this thing around.* It was a terrible miscalculation. It was intended to pit evangelicals against Roman Catholics. Obviously, it didn't work, and it probably doomed his campaign.

Parshall Well, your name was brought up again—this time by Vice President Gore, the man who wants to be the next president of the United States, speaking to a group of reporters. He said that George W. Bush has met privately with Pat Robertson and Jerry Falwell. Then he said, "Let me break that code for you," and gave his interpretation of what that meeting was supposed to be about: that folks like you would be able to influence who should be sitting on the United States Supreme Court. It looks like your name is going to be dragged through the mud in the days to come—like you're still going to be the object of disdain.

Falwell   The vice president totally fabricated that story. There has never been—not recently, not ever—a meeting with Pat Robertson, Jerry Falwell, and George W. Bush present. We have never had a conference call together. We've never exchanged faxes or e-mails. The vice president totally fabricated that story, and with no shame whatever. And just as he did not invent the Internet, and just as *Love Story* was not modeled after his and Tipper's relationship, neither did this meeting occur.

Parshall   Dr. Falwell, in many parts of what would be considered evangelical America, some are saying, "See, this is exactly why we shouldn't participate in the political process." As one of the men who helped to found the Moral Majority, do you think that's right-headed thinking?

Falwell   Oh, absolutely not. When you consider that 20 percent of the electorate in Virginia and Washington state acknowledged themselves to be "religious right" in the primaries, and many more would simply say, "I'm a Bible-believing Christian." But when eight out of nine of those vote for George W. Bush in retaliation for the assault of Mr. McCain against evangelical Christian leaders, Christian conservatives are a segment that the Republican Party dare not exclude. The Republican Party, after the Reagan model, must put together fiscal conservatives, political conservatives, and social conservatives.

SOCIAL VS. ECONOMIC CONSERVATIVES: HAIRLINE FRACTURE OR SEISMIC EARTHQUAKE?

What Jerry Falwell said in his radio interview was crucial. The Republican Party will make a devastating mistake if it ignores evangelical Christians. Further, Christians will make a huge mistake if they do not try to build a meaningful coalition with other conservatives, even if they do not share our Judeo-Christian worldview on all of the social and moral issues.

Yet the two of us have lost track of the number of times we have been in a room filled with conservatives—yes, conservatives all—when, before too long, a San Andreas Fault begins to appear in the group.

On one side of the split are the social conservatives. These are the folks, many of them evangelical Christians, who are solidly pro-life, "family values" people. They, like we, believe that life is sacred and that abortion is legalized infanticide. They, like we, do not believe that government should legitimize, nor should it aid or abet, any configuration of "marriage" except the one which has held civilizations together for several thousand years and which reflects God's design: one man and one woman—period. Social conservatives believe that government should deal seriously with public pornography and indecency, and that government should recognize that religious freedom and spiritual values are constitutionally protected categories, as our Founding Fathers intended. We also believe, further, that public officials should do what they can to help families—but in any event they should do nothing to hurt families, and at the very least they should simply get out of the way so good parents can raise good children with substantial autonomy.

On the other side of the room are the economic conservatives.

They want limited government—particularly on issues of commerce, trade, and investment. By and large they want lower taxes and a tax structure that encourages (rather than discourages) private enterprise. Many of them adhere to traditional ideas of federalism, with the federal government waning in size and reach, and a commensurate transfer of political power away from the federal government and over to state and local government. Within the economic conservatives are an increasing number of libertarians, who believe that freedom of the individual is an absolute good—and the less government has to do with any of our lives, the better.

Of course, there are permutations and variations within these groups. But the divisions are there, and they are substantial. It would seem, based on our nonscientific experience, that while many social conservatives share the ideas of the economic conservatives, the reverse is not as often true.

Unless the leadership of the Republican Party can straddle both of these groups, it will lose elections. More important, if the Republican Party continues to question its moral center, it will lose the Christian conservatives who have given it philosophical definition and who have provided it with moral impetus. Ronald Reagan was able to do it, but he is gone. Strategists like Paul Weyrich did it—but he now seems to question whether, in light of our national decay, our national public policies can be effectively changed in the traditional ways by those who promote the Judeo-Christian ethic.

Christians follow a King, not a party. We should be adherents to the eternal principles of Scripture more than mere party platforms. If the causes that we believe reflect the one true kingdom—the City of God, as Augustine described it—are not championed by the Republicans who would build the city of man, then it is time for us to leave. We need to note the Log Cabin Republicans, who promote the homosexual agenda. We need to note the pro-choice Republicans, who express their personal opposition to abortion yet will lift no finger to restrict it or outlaw it. Is this the new direction of the Grand Old Party? If so, it has ceased to be grand and has lost its moral authority to address the great issues of the day. The City of God is not the city of man, of course. But the city of man will never survive—let alone flourish—as long as it holds in willful contempt the principles of the eternal kingdom.

These new Republicans warn us that divisive and "emotionally charged" moral issues should not only be put on the back burner, but they should be taken out of the kitchen altogether. Yet, in so doing, they are betraying the important lessons of history. In fact, they are denying the moral heritage of the Republican Party.

OUT OF HUMAN BONDAGE

Ironically, the Republican Party was birthed because of an intense moral issue driving an equally profound social and political debate. In that sense, history is repeating the truth that divisions between church and state, and the distinctions drawn between spiritual conviction and political principle, are always up for debate.

The original organizational plans for the Republican Party were drawn up at the First Congregational Church in Ripon, Wisconsin, on February 28, 1854. The Republican Party began with disenchanted former members of the Whig Party, Free Soilers, and northern Democrats. They all had one thing in common: they were committed to stopping the spread of slavery and convinced that the existing political parties lacked the resolve or the conscience to do it.

Their first attempt at presidential politics failed in the election of 1856. Republicans nominated John C. Fremont, the celebrated military officer and explorer, whose motto was "free speech—free men—free territory," but he lost to Democrat James Buchanan.

By the next election, in 1864, the tide had turned. Abraham Lincoln, staunchly opposed to the expansion of slavery, won the presidential election as a Republican.

The parallels between the slavery debate in the last half of the nineteenth century and the abortion debate in the last half of the twentieth century have often been noted. But it is worth noting again, particularly because of the critical role evangelical Christians played in the abolitionist movement and the necessary role evangelicals must continue to play in opposing abortion.

The controversies over slavery and abortion share several common elements. In the 1800s in America, slavery proponents had a powerful economic incentive to continue the trade. The southern slave-holding states provided a full two-thirds of the world's cotton. They argued that the end of slavery would mean an end to much of the financial base of the southern states. In our age, the abortion industry tries to downplay the exploitative profits it has made at the expense of human life. However, the profits are in the billions. Carol Everett, now a born-again pro-lifer, used to own and operate a string of abortion clinics in Texas. She currently travels around the country sharing her experience and describing the wealth she amassed in her previous bloody business. The other economic aspect of the abortion debate has to do with the women and couples who seek abortion on economic grounds. A nine-month pregnancy, and the interruption it brings to job and career, is one of the major motivations to abort a baby.

There is also a *legal* parallel between the debates over slavery and abortion. One of the fulcrums of outrage in the slavery question was a decision of the Supreme Court, with Roger Taney presiding, that would help split the nation. The Dred Scott case involved a slave who had been taken to the state of Missouri (a slave state subject to the Missouri Compromise) to live with his slaveholder, but who had previously resided in free Illinois and the free territory of Wisconsin. Nevertheless, the Court ruled that the slave had no Fourteenth Amendment right to be recognized as a person. Instead, the slave was "property" and had to be returned to the slaveholder from the slave state. That decision was particularly ironic because Justice Taney, as a young trial lawyer, had once passionately (and successfully) represented a minister charged with inciting an insurrection that followed closely after one of his sermons that called for the freeing of slaves.

Today, even more than twenty years after the fact, the decision in *Roe v. Wade*, like the decision in *Scott v. Sandford*, continues to polarize the nation. It also continues to form the legal justification for the denial of human status to an entire human population.

But perhaps the closest parallel between these two issues is the way in which the moral and spiritual arguments have unfolded on each side. In the slavery debate a full one-fourth of the southern population held *some* slaves. That made it an overriding matter of moral convenience to find justifications (some of them based on a wrenching of the meaning of certain Bible passages) to avoid a wholesale disruption of ordinary life in the South. In the abortion debate the necessity of personal convenience (the vast majority of abortions have always been for mere convenience) dictated the argument that a fetus was not a person until it was born. This situation is like the slave who was not truly free until the unlikely time that his owner should drop him off on the other side of a free state. In essence, like the slaveholder, the pregnant mother holds all the cards until the very end.

But like the abortion debate of today, the abolitionist movement of 140 years ago was fueled by Christian (and particularly evangelical) fervor.

Three main groups populated the abolitionist position. First there were the Garrisonians (named after William Lloyd Garrison), who were the anarchists and radicals who held no particular religious beliefs (or if they did, they were anti-established church). Another group was the "political abolitionists," who were looking for an incremental, political solution out of the slavery debacle. Yet the third group, the Christian evangelicals, was the most significant. Evangelicals accounted for a higher percentage of the leadership of the abolitionist movement than any other group.[3]

The evangelicals in the positions of abolitionist leadership were much like the conservative evangelicals of today. They weren't considered "Unitarians, Universalists, or Liberals." They were almost all from denominations (Congregational, Methodist, Baptist, and Presbyterian) which, in the last half of the nineteenth century, were expressly orthodox in their belief—holding to the inerrancy of Scripture, the need for salvation through spiritual regeneration by a personal faith commitment to Jesus Christ as the Son of God, and the acceptance of His finished work on the cross.[4]

Princeton historian James McPherson notes the significant contribution of the evangelical Church in opposing slavery:

> The anticlericalism of Garrisonian abolitionists has obscured the importance of evangelical Protestantism in

the antislavery movement. The revivals of the Second Great Awakening left in their wake an army of reformers on the march against sin, especially the sin of slavery.[5]

Nor was evangelical opposition limited just to the northern states. One judge in Chatham County, Georgia, as far back as 1804, warned a grand jury under his charge that the curse of slavery was the work of men, not of God. He urged the jury to consider gradual but eventual emancipation, civic education, and Christian instruction for every former slave.[6] In 1830 a pamphlet entitled *An Address to the People Of North Carolina on the Evils of Slavery* was circulated by the Manumission Society. It declared slavery to be "contrary to the plain and simple maxims of Christian Revelation, or religion of Christ."[7] During the slavery debates in Virginia, Philip A. Bolling, a Piedmont area delegate to the state legislature, voiced the observation that "This, sir, is a Christian community. They read in their Bibles 'do unto all men as you would have them do unto you'—and this golden rule and slavery are hard to reconcile.[8]

In 1832 Mary Blackford of Fredericksburg, Virginia, was an active abolitionist. Her house was across the street from a slave trader. She learned that he was planning to sell a young male slave and had refused to allow the slave's mother to come and visit him. Blackford approached the trader and demanded that he permit the mother to have her final good-byes before the boy's departure. But the slave trader would not relent. Blackford later wrote, "I fixed my eyes steadily upon the hard-hearted being before me and asked him if he did not fear the judgments of an offended God." She would further note in her diary, "I am convinced that the time will come when we shall look back and wonder how Christians could sanction slavery."[9] Mary Blackford also ran a clandestine Sunday school for slaves, even though that practice was outlawed and carried with it the possibility of imprisonment. She was threatened on two occasions by a grand jury for teaching the Bible to slave children.

The evangelical church revolutionized the abolitionist movement, which ultimately brought slavery to an end. It marched arm in arm with the newly formed Republican Party—the party that stood for moral reform in a strife-torn nation. Now, slightly more than 140 years after the birth of that party, new issues of civil liberty and moral stability confront it.

At the meeting of the Republican National Committee in Indian Wells, California, in January 1998, the abortion issue again tested the moral tensile strength of the Republican Party. The Committee rejected, by an overwhelming vote of 114 to 43, a proposal to withhold party money from candidates who do not oppose late-term abortions. House Speaker and key Republican figure Newt Gingrich refused to take a position on the resolution. The party chairman, Jim Nicholson, took the unusual step of spearheading the effort to defeat the resolution. Only a few prominent Republicans were willing to publicly support the measure, including Congressman Henry Hyde, who gave an impassioned speech accusing the majority of giving only lip service to the pro-life cause.

The "new face" of Republicanism is well represented by William Weld, former governor of Massachusetts. During his controversial leadership in that state, Weld became the first governor in the nation to create a special task force on "gay and lesbian youth." In an op-ed in the *New York Times,* he presented a frontal attack on the pro-life initiative, sponsored by Republican Committeeman Tim Lambert, defeated by the party. Weld characterized the notion that the Republican Party should withdraw funding from candidates who do not oppose late-term abortions as "a rabid insistence on party discipline" that is more in line with "the Marxist tradition" than with American politics.[10] His astounding comparison of the defense of babies in the third trimester to Marxism is mind-boggling, yet it shows how the party that was created to outlaw human bondage is threatened by a new kind of ideological bondage.

Meanwhile, prohomosexual Log Cabin Republicans continue to garner influence in the Republican Party. Most audacious of all is the letterhead logo they have chosen for their organization: a picture of Abraham Lincoln graces the upper left corner of their official stationery. Using Lincoln, the champion of the moral imperative, as the symbol of American sexual decadence would be comical if it were not so tragic.

Christians have a unique opportunity to call Republicanism back to its roots. We must insist that Republicans learn to distinguish those areas that can be compromised from those that must not. We must refuse to create unprincipled "middle ground" when the issue is as fundamental as the right to life. As usual, it is hard to improve on the eloquence of Abraham Lincoln:

> Let us stand by our duty, fearlessly and effectively. Let us be diverted by none of those sophisticated contrivances wherewith we were so industriously plied and belabored— contrivances such as groping for some middle ground between the right and the wrong, vain as the search for a man who should be neither a living man nor a dead man.[11]

15 The Democratic Party: Is This Donkey Heading for Jerusalem?

CHRISTIANS WHO TAKE an activist role in impacting their communities through the Democratic Party have a tough row to hoe. They stand to lose both ways. First, if they believe there is any legitimacy to the idea of a party platform (that idea seems to be slowly drowning in a sea of political desperation), they will probably get the shivers after reading the philosophy of their party.

Take a close look at some of the current "rules of the road" for the Democratic Party. The 1996 Democratic National Platform stated, on the one hand, that "we want an America that is coming together around our enduring values, instead of drifting apart." Yet the same document declares: "The Democratic Party stands behind the right of every woman to choose [abortion], consistent with *Roe v. Wade*, and *regardless of ability to pay*."

What this simple sentence means is that not only does the Democratic Party want the full force of *Roe* to continue, but they want to force you, and me, to pay for the abortions of low-income women through our tax dollars.

In a current position paper, the Democratic Party has also supported:

- Expansion of federal employment discrimination laws to also protect the "sexual orientation" of each employee.

- President Clinton's decision to abolish considerations of "sexual orientation" in granting or denying national security clearances. (Formerly, the CIA denied security clearances if the fact of a person's homosexuality might make him more vulnerable to blackmail or extortion or might in some other way compromise his ability to protect national secrets.)

- Political asylum for gays and lesbians who are mistreated in their foreign countries of origin. (By contrast, the Clinton administration has opposed political asylum for those who fled communist China because of its policy of forced abortions.)

Second, if our Democratic brethren hop onto the Republican ship, then they are criticized, once again, for aligning the cross too closely with just one political party. Groups like Americans United for the Separation of Church and State often levy the criticism that evangelicalism is a wholly-owned subsidiary of the Republican Party. On that point evangelicals like Cal Thomas are now joining in this football-style "piling on" after the whistle is blown. In a strange way it is a little like the quandary a believer faces when a once vibrant and biblically correct church or denomination starts to show obvious signs of moral corruption and spiritual compromise. What do you do? Do you stay on the sinking ship and try to save it? Or do you leap for your life because it is too far gone?

There is no biblical slide rule that gives us a pat answer for that question. On the other hand, there are some basic principles we can rely on. The concept of "separation" from things that are clearly and unambiguously evil is a central theme in Scripture. In 2 Corinthians 6 Paul asked the church at Corinth:

> For what partnership have righteousness and lawlessness, or what fellowship has light with darkness? Or what harmony has Christ with Belial, or what has a believer in common with an unbeliever? Or what agreement has the temple of God with idols? For we are the temple of the living God; just as God said,
>
> "I WILL DWELL IN THEM AND WALK AMONG THEM; / AND I WILL BE THEIR GOD, AND THEY SHALL BE MY PEOPLE. / THEREFORE, COME OUT FROM THEIR MIDST AND BE SEPARATE," says the Lord. / "AND DO NOT TOUCH WHAT IS UNCLEAN; / And I will welcome you. / And I will be a father to you, / And you shall be sons and daughters to Me," / Says the Lord Almighty. (vv. 14–18)

We have deliberately left out the first part of the first verse quoted above for a reason. The questions Paul posed were really rhetorical. The answer was obvious, and it is contained in verse 14: "Do not be bound together with unbelievers . . ."

Has the Democratic Party become so morally bankrupt in its principles and agenda that the believer becomes defiled by associating with it? This is a critical question that must be answered before we walk into a voting booth the next time. It has to be answered before we give another dollar to another political campaign. And it must be answered before we agree to serve as a delegate to the Democratic convention or decide to run for public office.

Bible scholars Colin Brown and Hans-George Link have done a good job analyzing the original Greek word for *bound together* (sometimes translated *unequally yoked together*) Paul used in verse 14. Brown and Link give us a helpful evaluation of some of the subtle, but important, distinctions believers must make in their associations:

> The believer may not, however, eat at a table in an idol's temple (1 Cor. 8:10 f.). Paul may become all things to all men (1 Cor. 9:21 f.), but not to the point of partaking of the Lord's Supper and the table of demons (1 Cor. 10:21). The believer may eat with an unbeliever, but he should not knowingly eat meat that has been sacrificed to idols (1 Cor. 10:27 ff.). He should not give offence to Jew or Greek, if he can avoid it (1 Cor. 10:32) . . . Believers are to remain in the world and seek to win it. But they are not to allow their faith to be compromised in any way, particularly by pagan idolatry and the sexual mores of the heathen.[1]

By getting into a "double harness" with the philosophy of the Democratic Party, does the Christian bind himself or herself with that which is essentially at odds with the living God? Viewing at least the national agenda of that party, the burden of proof is on the believer who thinks that the ship can be saved. It is one thing for the hull to have a hole that can be patched. It is another for the ship to be guided by captains who are blinded to the lights that should guide them, and who follow a map that seems to have been drafted by the committees of the Prince of Darkness.

Yet we are also reminded of the work of a good friend of ours. Marv Munyon is a Bible-school trained preacher who decided to devote his life to running a pro-family legislative and educational effort. His office overlooks the state capitol in Madison,

Wisconsin. When he strolls through the galleries, halls, and legislative offices of that ornate building, Marv never hesitates to associate with any candidate or official who has the right view on the right issues, regardless of their political party. He often introduces his Democratic friends who have taken bold stands for truth as Bible-believing Christians to churches and pro-life groups. In the midst of controversial public issues, Marv has never alienated Democrats, publicly or privately, merely *because* they are *Democrats*.

In the end, the two of us have been convinced that the proper course is to seek the help and copartnership of *any* candidate or official, regardless of party affiliation, when he or she can do good for our communities, our nation, and our churches. That does not mean that we will necessarily endorse that candidate or embrace his or her party. But it does mean that we should stand ready to meaningfully coalesce with public officials across the political spectrum in order to save innocent human life, to protect our families or communities from government overreaching, and to build a firewall for our religious liberties.

16 | An Independent Party: Third Way or the Wrong Way?

THE 2000 PRESIDENTIAL campaign presented a number of different themes very early on. But one of the most consistent is the real talk (particularly among some Republicans) about creating a viable, conservative third party. Bob Smith, Republican senator from New Hampshire, was in the first lap of the race when he bolted from the Republican Party and declared himself to be an independent, only to return to the GOP in the end.

Pat Buchanan, a man with the credentials of a loyal and stalwart (though independent-minded) Republican, threw his hands up in disgust (again) when the Republican-controlled House of Representatives voted (again) to approve Most Favored Nation trade privileges to China. The vote came at the same time China was threatening war against Taiwan and showing new resolve to stamp out religious freedom in that communist nation. Buchanan declared: "Today's House vote makes me ashamed to be a Republican."[1] Early in the election Pat Buchanan indicated that he would not rule out running as an independent or on the ballot of a third party. Ultimately he decided to leave the Republican Party and run for the presidential candidacy of the Reform Party.

Indeed, third-party fever has been slowly building. Ross Perot's third-party bid, while never even close to the mark, was effective enough to capture disenchanted Republicans and sweep Bill Clinton into the White House. When the state of Minnesota elected a former professional wrestler named Jesse "The Body" Ventura, running as an independent, as governor of the Land of Ten Thousand Lakes, the media started taking notice. Not long afterward, Jesse Ventura became the man of ten thousand media interviews.

On closer examination, though, it becomes clear that Ross Perot's influence as the official agitator against the two-party system has been waning. As for Ventura, the factors that brought him to the statehouse were more complex than a simple rejection of the two reigning political parties. In addition to the usual "lesser of several evils" thinking and general voter disgust with party politics as usual, there was another factor. Like Wisconsin, its sister state to the east, Minnesota may be thought of as part of the mosaic of midwestern traditionalism; but, in fact, it has a strong eccentric streak. Wisconsin had a reputation of backing everything from far-right conservatives (Joseph McCarthy) to progressives, independents, and even socialists; Minnesota is a twin sister. Stated bluntly, Minnesota is no Iowa.

The Farmer-Labor Party, a third political party, was formed in Minnesota in 1920. By 1944 it became so powerful that it joined ranks with the Democratic Party, becoming the Democratic-Farmer-Labor Party (DFL). A politician of no less stature than Hubert Humphrey became its standard-bearer. In 1975 the state Republican Party renamed itself the Independent Republicans of Minnesota. Thus, the strong tendency of that state toward independent politics may have played a role in Ventura's victory.

The question of the legitimacy and credibility of the Reform Party is still an unanswered question, judging by its own luminaries. For example, it did not take Governor Ventura very long, to start making statements that have probably put his Minnesota constituents into a permanent state of cringe. In an interview in *Playboy* magazine, Ventura commented that he considered organized religion a crutch for weak, simple-minded people. Further, attracting possible candidates like casino builder Donald Trump as presidential hopefuls does nothing to raise the stature of the Reform Party as a serious political force.

The question of a conservative third party is not idle chatter for evangelical Christians. It has been in the wind from the time of Pat Robertson's presidential run, and it resurfaces with each expression of disappointment in the Republican Party by evangelical leaders. But for evangelicals it cannot merely be a question of politics or strategy. If our freedoms of self-governance are blessings from God, then they must be used as any other form of wise stewardship. Likewise, the principles of practical wisdom found in Scripture can give us much guidance in exercising this stewardship.

We find an abundance of evidence that God calls us to practical and realistic wisdom. When our Lord discussed the way we should live in the light of His coming, He urged us to effectively multiply our resources and the blessings we have from Him (Matt. 25:14–30). We are called by Paul to conduct ourselves "with wisdom toward outsiders, making the most of the opportunity" (Col. 4:5). The values of diligent planning and careful strategy are recognized in Scripture: "The plans of the diligent lead surely to advantage / But everyone who is hasty comes surely to poverty" (Prov. 21:5). Effective, efficient, and intelligent use of our civil freedoms is a critically important obligation.

David Barton, a well-known Christian historian and an astute political observer, had some interesting comments on this issue when he was a guest on the July 14, 1999 broadcast of *Janet Parshall's America*. Some of his answers go against the "popular wisdom" believers in Christ sometimes follow in pledging allegiance to a third party:

Parshall   Today, Phyllis Schlafly put out a press release saying that George W. Bush has never asked the conservative movement for support, and that Bob Smith's departure from the Republican Party should be a wake-up call to the Republican establishment. A wake-up call is a good thing, but winning is the goal here. So, can you do it in a third party?

Barton   Well, if we do it this time, it will be the first time in history. Third parties do not do well, even if they have huge people at the top. Teddy Roosevelt, after serving two terms as president, ran a third party and didn't even get noticed. When Roosevelt moved over to the Bull Moose Party, that was the end of it. You have people who were huge in history like William Work, who served with Washington. And Adams and Jefferson, who with the attorney general of the United States moved over to the Anti-Masonic Party, and didn't carry the nomination of any state except Vermont. Furthermore, when [third parties] have been introduced, it has forced greater compromises than were necessary with only two players at the table. The more people you inject into the equation, the more you have to compromise because no one has a real majority anymore.

Parshall   Let's go back to recent history, to what we call the Perot Factor. Bill Clinton's victory has to be clearly ascribed to Ross Perot, who gave Bill Clinton the White House.

Barton   If people were wanting to make a statement of conscience [by voting for Perot], they certainly did. And now we still have partial-birth abortions. We still have homosexual rights moving down a fast agenda. If the intent was to make a message for clear conscience, they really accomplished exactly the opposite.

Parshall   You and I both believe that it needs to continually be principle over politics. But somehow you need to ask yourself, What is the principled thing to do when you have a system that—sorry, like it or not, folks—is strongly two-party?

Barton   That's really the key. We may have wished, in a card game, that we'd been dealt a different set of cards. But you play with what you've been dealt. And what we have been dealt is a two-party system. I was just down in one of the southern states, where folks were saying "Look, I just could not vote for Dole in good conscience, so I stayed home." I said, "Okay, I can handle that. Dole wasn't a good candidate. But I want you to tell me how you're going to stand before God on Judgment Day and say, 'I had this great opportunity

219

to vote against a guy who supported partial-birth abortions, who was supporting homosexual rights, who was into all the things You're against, but I knew You wouldn't want me to do that, so I just stayed home.'" It makes no sense that we had the opportunity to at least slow the path of evil, and we said, "Well, I don't want to do that, because the guy I could vote for to help slow the path of evil is not really who I want."

Before we cast our votes for unelectable candidates in the final elections—before we throw our precious liberty aside to vote into the mere "protest" category—we would be wise to remember the words of one of our founding fathers, John Adams. To him the vote was not just an empty American ceremony. Rather, it represented a precious privilege quite unique in the history of the world. Adams noted "how few of the human race have ever enjoyed an opportunity of making an election of government for themselves and their children."[2] Perhaps it is time for evangelicals to realize that our votes *do* count. Otherwise, we have no right to complain when they count the votes.

WHAT WE CAN LEARN FROM THE INDEPENDENTS

Regardless of whether we have a party affiliation, evangelicals ought to take notice of the current trend toward independent parties in America. It is telling us something about ourselves and about where our culture is heading; this trend ought to be considered a valuable barometer.

Washington, D.C. is an establishment town. While the faces change, many of the institutions that broker the power become entrenched and tend to outlast the presidential administrations and congressional personalities that come and go. Yet even in this establishment town, things have been changing in a very fundamental way.

Let us remember, first, that Bill Clinton was elected on the premise that he was from "outside the Beltway" of Washington politics. He appeared on MTV and played his saxophone. He said that he genuinely "felt" our "pain." He wanted us to think he was breaking the political mold. He acted like a Democrat but talked like a Republican. To an American public that had grown increasingly disillusioned with politics and politicians, Bill Clinton could cast himself in the role of the "nonpolitical" politician. Now, after two terms of President Bill Clinton, it is clear that he had more of the political creature in him than any president within recent memory. Yet his canonization as the "comeback kid" was really due, in a large degree, to his ability to cloak himself in the costume of the maverick, the outsider, the well-intentioned country boy in the big city—in other words, as an ideological independent.

Even the think tanks that fuel the intellectual life of Washington are changing. One of the newest to cast itself in this role as "thinking person's independent think tank" is the New America Foundation. Its founder and CEO is thirty-something Ted Halstead, a graduate of the JFK School of Government at Harvard. He has made the rounds of D.C.-based talking-heads television shows and has received a glowing presence within the pages of the *Atlantic Monthly*. His appearance on the political scene could best be described as "Mr. Generation X Goes to Washington." Halstead had commented that some 35 percent of all Americans polled list themselves as politically independent. That percentage rises to 40 percent when we apply it to persons under forty years old, and 44 percent for Gen-Xers.

Yet Halstead's observations on the changing trends in America, particularly among the Generation X group (in their twenties and thirties, just out of college and into newly developing careers), are disconcerting. He conceded that "Xers have internalized core beliefs and characteristics that bode ill for the future of American democracy." He cited them as generally having a negative attitude toward America, having a heightened sense of materialism, and a lack of trust in relationships or traditional institutions.[3]

On one hand, this is disheartening information. It means that the next generation of voters will care about private property rights (particularly *their* property) but may not understand, nor wish to defend, the essentials of parental rights. It may mean that we will have a population that cares mostly about their own social security but not national security—who will care about public improvements catering to their comfort but not about the future of religious liberties.

On the other hand, this may be an auspicious opportunity for the evangelical Church. We can point out to this new demographic group that we share some things in common. For instance, the Christian must never make his allegiance to scriptural principles and ideals secondary to any political party. In that regard, we can empathize with an "independent" attitude. Further, we share a concern about placing absolute trust in government—though for different reasons. We know that any system of government that is not kept under tight control and that is not responsive to the will of the people can become a tool of tyranny. Understanding the way Gen-Xers view government can also present us with an opportunity to explain why the Judeo-Christian perspective is the only viable alternative.

After all, there are only two primary ways of viewing the possibility of a moral society. The first is to encourage everyone to pursue his or her own private self-interest and then hope that, collectively, all those self-interested efforts will combine to create a generally beneficial community. The fallacy comes in presuming that such a society will be a moral one, rather than simply one that maximizes benefits for most of us. In that kind of worldview, cruelly sacrificing the rights of the unfortunates (who are in the minority), if it would maximize the comfort and convenience of the majority, is always justifiable.

The other view is that right and wrong, justice and injustice, and concepts of the general welfare of a nation can only come from a moral understanding of the world—from a worldview that bases its social ethics on transcendent values. Such values tell us that even though it may be in my immediate self-interest to steal from you, if I am hungry and you have food, I cannot do that because those ethical principles are more important—and more binding on me—than my drive to fill my stomach. Self-interest, by contrast, only worries about the risk of being caught, or weighs the degree of punishment against the "benefit" of what I can steal.

Of all the value systems that make claims about human dignity and a respect for life, liberty, and the pursuit of happiness, none have fared better than the Christian consensus that birthed American democracy. The burden of proof is on those, therefore, who believe that some other value system—or no value system at all—will give us a better future.

17 | Beware the Political Co-opt

ELECTIONEERING FOR THE presidency had barely begun in 1999 when an interesting question was posed to presidential hopeful Al Gore. Vice President Gore had been struggling for months on how to approach the Monica Lewinsky scandal. During the impeachment hearings Gore vigorously defended President Clinton. Now that he was running for the White House, however, Gore was beginning to voice disappointment in Clinton's behavior.

In Hanover, New Hampshire, a citizen confronted Vice President Gore on his two inconsistent positions on the president's sexual immorality. Gore responded with a prime example of how politics can co-opt, and ultimately corrupt, Christian truth. He stated that his seemingly inconsistent positions were explained by his personal philosophy, which was to "hate the sin but love the sinner."[1]

This "philosophy," of course, is a common theme throughout the Bible, and a popular one among evangelicals. Which, is perhaps, why Mr. Gore chose to use it publicly in a campaign year.

But his exegesis of this biblical concept was distorted, at best.

The concept of "sinner versus sin" can be found, among other places, in Psalm 99:8, which states: "O LORD our God, Thou didst answer them; / Thou wast a forgiving God to them, / And yet an avenger of their evil deeds."

Mr. Gore chose to exercise his "forgiving" spirit when it would do Mr. Clinton the most political good. He then displayed the need for "avenging" the president's immorality when it would be to his political advantage but would do the nation no good at all (it came long after the Senate trial was over).

This technique of "political co-opt" has been around for a long time. There is a good argument to be made that Constantine's "conversion" to Christianity in A.D. 313 had more to do with insuring his military and political conquest of the Roman Empire than it did with having a heart that panted after God.

In an example familiar to many of us, England's King Henry VIII manipulated the archbishop of Canterbury to annul his marriage to Catherine of Aragon for his own personal and political gains. In the short run that permitted him to claim legitimacy for his secret marriage to Anne Boleyn, who was already pregnant with his child. In the long run it ended up contributing, quite at odds with King Henry's own personal Catholic beliefs, to the rise of the Church of England, and furthered the ultimate triumph of Protestantism in England.

To use a more obscure example, in the summer of the year 1000, Iceland was declared an officially Christian nation by the decree of the land's chief lawgiver. At that point in its history, Iceland was caught between the developing "new" religion of Christianity and the older pagan beliefs in the Viking gods. The fact remains, however, that the edict appears to have been due more to the need for national and political unity than as a result of any kind of spiritual revival.[2] The power brokers of ancient Iceland, like Henry VIII of England, found it expedient to use Christianity to forge a unified political base and to ensure stability.

In modern times, Bill Clinton has proved to be a master at the political use of religious symbolism. Case in point: the widely published photo of President Clinton leaving church on Sunday, not only with Bible in hand, but with the Bible raised coyly next to his head— as if to ensure that his face would be captured next to Holy Writ.[3]

A more blatant example occurred during the congressional battle over Bill Clinton's crime bill. The president appeared behind the pulpit of the Full Gospel A.M.E. Zion Church in Maryland, and before a crowd of two thousand implored Congress to "do the will of God" and pass his crime legislation without any amendments.[4]

On the other hand, presidents regularly (and somewhat ceremonially) pronounce the usual "God bless America" in their speeches, urge Americans to call on God (particularly in times of war or great social upheaval), make proclamations about the importance of the Bible, and participate in the National Day of Prayer. Evangelicals usually herald these examples of civic Christianity on the part of our elected officials. In light of this, why is Bill Clinton's declaration about God's will on the crime bill any different?

The difference lies, first, in the opportunity for ulterior political motive. Christians must understand that we can, and must, put the motives of political officials under scrutiny. This is different, however, from the kind of "judging" that the Scripture condemns. We are commanded: "Do not judge lest you be judged" (Matt. 7:1). This is different from the kind of biblical analysis we must bring to bear on those who lead us. In fact, Jesus presumed that His followers should and would be able to make moral and spiritual judgments about the world around them. After Jesus gave His warning about judging in Matthew 7:1, he then told his listeners:

> You hypocrite, first take the log out of your own eye, and then you will see clearly to take the speck out of your brother's eye. Do not give what is holy to dogs, and do not throw your pearls before swine, lest they trample them under their feet, and turn and tear you to pieces. (vv. 5–6)

In other words, we must first examine ourselves before we can effectively examine others. That is quite different from saying we should forego the business of examining the culture (or its leadership or spokespersons) altogether. As for the second verse above, Bible scholar Charles Ryrie makes the point that "the disciples were expected to make moral distinctions and not allow those who reject the invitation of Christ to treat precious things [*i.e.*, spiritual truths] as cheap."[5] When a political leader uses the parlance of spiritual truth, the Church must scrutinize that leader to see if he or she is thereby cheapening and degrading the content of Scripture merely to achieve a political advantage.

In the case of the crime bill and Bill Clinton, the president had a clear motive to use, for political purposes, religious language and symbolism. He wanted his legislation passed through Congress, and he said so from the pulpit of a church. His timing, and his shameless public appeal for churches to heed "God's will," made it clear that he wanted to influence a legislative vote through the pressure of churches (particularly African-American churches).

The second factor by which we must determine whether a spiritual appeal by a cultural or political leader is appropriate is how that public pronouncement fits into that person's overall cultural worldview or political philosophy. If we have a leader whose "walk matches his talk," or even whose "walk exceeds his talk," we have a right to be less suspicious of ulterior motives or manipulation. On the other hand, if the leader we are analyzing had adopted a personal philosophy that views spiritual truth merely as ammunition for firing the next political volley, we must cry out against this. In the case of President Clinton, we have reason to conclude that it springs from a well-developed, yet ruthless, political tradition that is almost three hundred years old.

Charles de Secondat, Baron de Montesquieu is the acknowledged forerunner of modern political philosophy. Born and raised in France in the final decades of the 1600s, he became an expert in law, a wide range of scientific subjects, and in the affairs of government. His personal attitudes and practices, however, ranged from the bizarre to the indecent. Preoccupied with the concept of love, yet himself a party to a rather loveless marriage, he authored some literature that is considered pornographic. He criticized both traditional monogamy as well as polygamy. Even more incredible, he found nothing negative to say—and much to be praised—for the practice of *incest.*

But in the field of politics, Montesquieu was a major influence. His *The Spirit of the Laws* is considered a classic of political philosophy and continues to have an enormous impact on modern notions of government. He is mentioned in the major textbooks on history, political science, and social theory.

In order to understand the intellectual origins of the recent Clintonesque co-opting of evangelical Christianity, we must go to Montesquieu. In *The Spirit of the Laws* he is crystal clear about the ways in which religion can be used in the political sphere. Montesquieu had little regard for traditional, Bible-based Christianity as a revealed theology. To him, such religious beliefs not only failed to present a solution to the dehumanization of mankind—in fact, such beliefs *caused* the dehumanization of humanity. The Bible, and those forms of worship that relied on it, had absolutely no value to him as a form of truth-claim about God. Religion, to Montesquieu, was simply a vested interest to use as a political tool.[6]

Yet as a vested interest in society, he wrote, Christianity had a *collective* power to reinforce that societal morality that best aided the political establishment. Therefore, Christianity is a great benefit to the political order, according to Montesquieu. In the end, for him almost *any* religion can be used successfully by the state, "because even a false religion is the best security we can have of the probity of men."[7]

When politicians look at the benefit of Christianity this way, no wonder it results in a morally skewed state of affairs. It is amazing that President Clinton vetoed the will of Congress to restrict partial-birth abortion on the same weekend he made a declaration recognizing National Children's Week. In the very Bible that the president carried prominently as he left his church, we see God's reward to the Jewish midwives who refused to be accomplices in the ancient equivalent of late-term, partial-birth abortions, even though that procedure had been commanded by the pharaoh (Ex. 1:15–22). While "God's will" about the pending crime bill is uncertain, it can be said fairly confidently that God had made His will known about partial-birth abortion. Because Bill Clinton has been repeatedly evaluated as, above all else, a political opportunist by his own former advisers and even his own supporters, his double standards about God's attitude on abortion tell us that there is a good chance that he is using religion as a mere political tool. The parallels between his philosophy and that of Montesquieu only corroborate this.

On the abortion issue, history gives us another stark illustration. While Montesquieu, a product of the early eighteenth century, is usually touted as a great example of Enlightenment thinking on matters of liberty and is quite Clintonesque (interestingly, he believed that the greatest civic virtue was tolerance), his view on the question of the right to life was also surprisingly, and disturbingly, modern. While referring to the ancient practice of "exposing" unwanted infants (the practice of infanticide where a newborn would be set out to die by exposure to the elements of nature) this is what he said: "The Roman policy was very good in respect to the exposing of children . . . If the infants were deformed and monstrous [the emperor] permitted the exposing [of] them, after having shown them to five of their nearest neighbors."[8]

Those who, like Montesquieu, are the likeliest to use religion *merely* as a support system for their political campaign or social philosophy, and nothing more, can at the same time be the quickest to tolerate even the most hideous violation of biblical values.

When a political candidate or official, of whatever party or persuasion, attempts to use evangelical Christians as a political football, or the Bible as a field goal extra point, we must scrutinize his or her ulterior motives. When these spiritual professions by our leaders do not match up with moral atrocities in other areas, we have a duty to cry "foul." If we fail to do this, we fail to fulfill this prophetic calling of the church: not to *foretell* future events like the prophets of old, but to *forthtell* the eternal principles of God's Word as applied to current issues of the day.

Conclusion

ON NOVEMBER 21, 1620, an old wine ship called the *Mayflower*, which had been converted into a passenger carrier for a collective of religious dissenters, was making its way across the Atlantic Ocean. Frighteningly tiny by today's standards, this vessel had already been out to sea for two months. The passengers were almost all Calvinist Christians, mostly English citizens, though some had been exiled to Holland. Their leaders were William Bradford and William Brewster.

Having braved most of the journey across the ocean, and having survived the ravages of the elements from without, the passengers now faced a challenge of equal measure from dissension within. The harrowing and seemingly endless ocean journey, the cramped quarters, and the deep deprivation of basic physical comforts had finally led to harsh disagreements on board the ship. How, then, could they manage their 80,000-acre tract of land in this new colony that they had purchased from the Virginia Company—indeed, how could they manage their new community at all, in light of the conflicts that were brewing in their ranks before they had even landed?

The solution was found in the drafting of a remarkable document. It was a charter of first principles that reminded the religious dissenters of the goal of their mission. It also called for an equal measure of commitment from all of them to its achievement. We know this document today as the Mayflower Compact. This concise yet profound charter stated:

> In the name of God, Amen. We, whose names are underwritten, the loyal subjects of our dread sovereign Lord, King James, by the grace of God . . . having undertaken, for the *glory of God, and the advancement of the Christian faith*, and the honor of our king and country, a voyage to plant the first colony in the Northern parts of Virginia, do by these presents solemnly and mutually in the presence of God, and one another, covenant and combine ourselves together into *a civil body politic*, for our better ordering and preservation and furtherance of the ends aforesaid; and . . . to *enact . . . such just and equal laws . . .* as shall be thought most meet and convenient for the general good of the Colony . . .

This Compact bears three essential elements that are just as binding on Christians today as they were on our spiritual ancestors, the Pilgrims.

First, it articulated a clear *spiritual purpose.* The founding of those "Northern parts of Virginia" (the area which is now Massachusetts) was not just for king and country. The founding of this new nation was primarily "for the glory of God, and the advancement of the Christian faith." All that we do—whether in politics, in pure street evangelism, or in writing an article on cultural matters for an academic journal—must be for the purpose of advancing the Christian faith.

Second, the Compact recognized the pragmatic need for a "civil body politic"; in other words, it accepted the importance of *political structures* as not incompatible with the Christian faith. Institutional government and political groups are necessary for order, peace, and the preservation of freedom, and particularly for the "furtherance of the ends" of advancing of the message of Jesus Christ.

Lastly, this document declared that the means of achieving those goals would include the enactment of *provisions of law*— of "just and equal laws . . . for the general good." Lawmaking was viewed as part of not only the temporal order but also the spiritual order of things.

It is interesting how, 167 years later, a delegation of American statesmen at the Constitutional Convention drafted a preamble that appears so closely to mirror the Mayflower Compact's first principles:

> We the people of the United States, in order to form a more perfect union, establish justice, insure domestic tranquility, provide for the common defense, promote the general welfare, and secure the blessings of liberty for ourselves and our posterity, do ordain and establish this Constitution for the United States of America.

Gone, of course, were the declarations of the "glory of God" and the "advancement of the Christian faith." Instead, our founders framed the First Amendment, later added to the Constitution, which demonstrated that as the very first principle, out of all the first principles of freedom, is the concept of freedom of religion: "Congress shall make no law respecting an establishment of religion, or prohibiting the free exercise thereof."

Thus, we are free, at least in theory if not in practice, to show forth the glory of God and to advance the Christian faith across the breadth of this great land by zealously enjoying "the free exercise" of our spiritual mission. If we are not influencing the land of our forefathers, it is probably due to one of only two things. Either we are *choosing* not to freely exercise our Christian influence effectively and zealously, or we have been *restrained* from doing so by a hostile culture. Yet given our freedom to participate in our own self-governance, regardless of which is true (and even if both are true), the fault lies with us. The indictment rests at the door of the Church. In America, God has given us a great and noble stewardship of freedom and self-rule. The question for the twenty-first century is whether we will squander it, like Esau of old, for the comforts of a pot of stew and a full belly.

Those who call for a reversal of Christian activism because of our "failures" in the secular realm might as well castigate the Pilgrims of Plymouth Rock. After all, nearly half of them died during the first winter. It is hard to imagine a worse catastrophe for a new "body politic" than the inability to ensure the survival of half of its population. Instead, however, we declare them to be heroes and patriots. We do so because we now know, in the warm comfort of our climate-controlled homes and within a few steps of well-stocked refrigerators, that it all turned out all right for their "posterity"—which is all of us, their successors. Success, it seems, is not capable of being defined unless we know where to locate the finish line.

If we are to frame an appropriate compact for the Church in the new millennium, we first must be able to locate the finish line. Unless we do that, we will be blinded by illusions of success, only to find that we have been chasing the world's mirages. Or we will miss the real spiritual fruits of our efforts, because we forgot that eternal truths are not measured with yardsticks made of wood. The finish line for the Christian is not in the political victory lap. It is not in Washington, D.C. or in any capital of any state in the Union. It is not in Congress or the Supreme Court or the city council, even though we should wage our struggles there for those things that are right, and true, and reflective of God's order of things. The finish line is at the gate of the City of God. Our duty is not to tally the votes for God—our duty is to be faithful to Him in the sphere of influence to which we are called.

What we need to remember, then, is to run the race, but that we will realize "victory" only when we get to the finish line, and not before. Our race ends at the great gate of the City of God, and not one inch short of that.

Until then we must shed His light within the cities of man. We must do so because it is what the Lord Jesus did when He walked the roads of ancient Galilee. He did not separate spiritual truth from political or cultural truth. While He made the distinction between Caesar and God, it was only because obedience to the former was but a function of the higher duty of obedience to the latter.

As life in the cities of this world seems to grow darker and the process of moral decision making becomes more confusing, it is inviting to look for superspiritualized avenues of escape. The walls of our houses of worship will become more comfortable than those noisy and irreverent (and even dangerous) marketplaces where ideas are debated and cultural policy is forged. But because bad ideas can have tragic implications, and because dangerous policy can lead to destruction, we must not be silent and we must not be passive. Neither can Christians afford to become cloistered in enclaves of self-congratulation. And while potluck suppers in the church basement have their honored place in the ministry of service, we cannot live out the twenty-first century in our church basements.

We do not, as followers of Christ, have the option of either isolating ourselves entirely within the cocoon of the Church or throwing ourselves blindly into all of the pursuits and battles of the world. Jesus did not give us that kind of choice. He called us to be of a *heavenly character* while penetrating the cities and kingdoms that are patterned after the *character of the world.*

In His well-known Sermon on the Mount, the Lord Jesus gave us this commission:

> You are the light of the world. A city set on a hill cannot be hidden. Nor do men light a lamp, and put it under the peck-measure, but on the lampstand; and it gives light to all who are in the house. Let your light shine before men in such a way that they may see your good works, and glorify your Father who is in heaven. (Matt. 5:14–16)

As we traverse the market squares of commerce, the courtrooms and halls of government, the centers of media and communication, and the academic, artistic, scientific, and cultural enclaves of this world, we are commissioned to shine the light of the gospel throughout—in both the palaces of power and the mean streets of poverty.

This certainly means that we are to be nothing *less* than traditionally evangelistic in our lifestyle and our message. But it also means that we are to be considerably *more* than that. The "light" we share, which is the whole truth of the whole gospel, is intertwined with our "good works." Our good works, in turn, are to be of such a nature as to necessarily glorify our Father in the sight of the world. Nowhere in this Scripture do we find Jesus demanding that our good works *only* be of a private, individualistic, and nonpolitical nature. Our representative democracy was not granted to us by mistake. Rather, it is a blessing—a stewardship of freedom—from God. Given that fact, it is both right and proper that the Church, as it pursues its grand mission of the Great Commission, be involved in both the quiet and individual works of personal charity and kindness, as well the more public works of righteousness, justice, truth telling, and the preservation of freedom.

These kind of good works must be active, positive, and above all—*penetrating*. In the verse preceding Matthew 5:14, where Jesus calls us to the task of being "the light of the world," he also calls us to be "the salt of the earth." Salt and light have at least one property in common: they both have a penetrating influence on the condition to which they are applied. When a city is penetrated with light, its darkness fades into the shadows. When meat is preserved with salt, it no longer is susceptible to decay. When we bring His light to bear in the cities of man, we work and pray for the retreat of both darkness and decay.

Even though our goal is to stand for truth in matters of public policy and public interest in such a way that men may glorify the heavenly Father, this does not mean that we have failed when we are met with opposition or even condemnation. In fact, our Lord told us to expect exactly that.

Just before He gave His disciples the *commission* to be salt and light, He gave them the *expectation* of persecution: "Blessed are you when men cast insults at you, and persecute you, and say all kind of evil against you falsely, on account of Me. Rejoice, and be glad, for your reward in heaven is great, for so they persecuted the prophets who were before you" (Matt. 5:11–12).

In the end, then, living out our dual citizenship between earthly kingdoms and the heavenly one will always be a daily challenge. Like riding a bicycle, juggling duties of home and work, being both parent and spouse, or mastering those other truly important but frustrating exercises of equilibrium, we will succeed only by practicing and attempting to achieve balance. As the Church continues to be engaged in the cultural debates and struggles of the twenty-first century, we must pray—and expect—that it will achieve, through committed practice, a better sense of balance in maintaining its dual citizenship. One thing, however, is clear: Believers will not learn to balance their dual citizenship by pretending that they have only one, rather than two, kingdoms to worry about. Though we should seek the kingdom of Christ first (Matt. 6:33), we should not avoid the mandate to do what is good and true in the kingdoms of man.

Admittedly, however, though we commit ourselves to lighting the darkened corners of the cities of our present world, we do so with an unquenchable yearning. The weary traveler who knocks off his shoes and enjoys the hearth of a friendly hotel room knows that, for all its comforts, that place is still not home. Home is somewhere else.

At the end of the day, we Christians should still yearn for that City whose builder is the Lord Himself. One day our task within this earthly jurisdiction will be finished, and we will no longer be called to carry the light. Instead, our task then will be to live in the presence of the Light. How glorious will be the King of that heavenly city, and how blessed we will be to live in His presence!

Notes

Introduction

1. Tomas B. Endsall, "Key Conservative Surrenders in Culture War, but Fight Continues," *Washington Post*, 18 February 1999, A06; Tom Strode, Ethics and Religious Liberty Commission/Southern Baptist Convention, press release, 25 February 1999.

2. Paul M. Weyrich, "Separate and Free," *Washington Post*, 7 March 1999, Outlook section.

3. David Von Drehle, "Social Conservatives' Ties to GOP Fraying," *Washington Post*, 28 February 1999, A-1.

4. Cal Thomas and Ed Dobson, *Blinded by Might* (Grand Rapids, MI: Zondervan, 1999), 142.

5. Ibid., 117.

6. "Is the Religious Right Finished?" *Christianity Today*, 6 September 1999, 43–55.

7. Patrick Goodenough, CNS London Bureau Chief, "Southern Baptists Clash with White House Over Religious Intolerance," CNS New.com, 27 December 1999.

Chapter 1

1. Richard Weaver, *Ideas Have Consequences* (Chicago: University of Chicago Press, 1948), 12–13.

2. Edward O. Wilson, "The Two Hypotheses of Human Meaning," *The Humanist*, September–October 1999, 31.

3. Barbara Olson, *Hell to Pay: The Unfolding Story of Hillary Rodham Clinton* (Washington, D.C.: Regnery, 1999), 45–46, 50.

4. Saul D. Alinsky, *Rules for Radicals* (New York: Vintage Books, 1971), title page.

5. Ibid., 62.

6. Thomas D. Elias, "Vice President Visits Los Angeles Gays and Lesbians," *Washington Times*, 25 June 1999, A8.

7. Jeremy Rabkin, "The Culture War That Isn't," *Policy Review*, August–September 1999, 18.

8. James Davison Hunter, *Culture Wars: the Struggle to Define America* (New York: Basic Books, 1991), 325.

9. Tom Sine, *Cease-Fire: Searching for Sanity in America's Culture Wars* (Grand Rapids, MI: William B. Eerdmans Publishing, 1995), 156–157, 167.

10. *Reno v. American Civil Liberties Union*, 521 U.S. 844 (1997).

11. Dick Armey, "American Bigotry," excerpted in *World*, 16 October 1999, 32.

Chapter 2

1. Wayne W. Dyer, *Your Sacred Self* (New York: Harper Collins, 1995), 254.

2. Cheryl Wetzstein and Ralph Z. Hallon, "Clinton Lashes Out at Religious Conservatives," *Washington Times*, 25 June 1994, A1.

3. Dan Balz, "Democrat Fazio Assails Religious Right in GOP," *Washington Post*, 22 June 1994, A4.

4. David Frum, "Myth of the Religious Right," *USA Today*, 25 July 1999, 11A.

5. Robert Booth Fowler, Allen D. Hertzke, and Laura R. Olson, *Religion and Politics in America* (Boulder, CO: Westview Press, 1999), 155.

6. Joanne Beard and Washington Education Association, *If You Don't They Will—A Political Guide for Successful School Support* (1989), 47.

7. Francis Schaeffer, *The Great Evangelical Disaster* (Westchester, IL: Crossway Books, 1984), 144.

8. Walter Wink, *The Powers That Be: Theology for a New Millenium* (New York: Galilee Doubleday, 1998), back cover.

9. Ibid., 162.

10. Jim Wallis, *The Soul of Politics* (New York: The New Press/Orbis Books of Mary Knoll, 1994), foreword.

11. *Recovering the Evangel*, by the editors of *Sojourners*, no. 1 (undated), 5.

12. Tom Sine, "A Hijacked Heritage," *Recovering the Evangel*, by the editors of *Sojourners*, no. 1 (undated), 17.

13. *Recovering the Evangel*, by the editors of *Sojourners*, no. 1 (undated), 5.

14. Wallis, *The Soul of Politics*, 36–37.

15. Ibid., 36.

16. From the speaker biographies given at Interfaith Alliance press conference, 15 September 1999, Washington, D.C. (www.interfaithalliance.org).

17. Statement of Rev. Dr. C. Welton Gaddy, Interfaith Alliance press conference, 15 September 1999, Washington, D.C.

18. Ibid., statement of Sister Mary Carol Bennett.

19. Ibid., statement of Rev. Dr. C. Welton Gaddy.

20. Dennis L. Okholm and Timothy R. Philipps, eds., *More Than One Way?—Four Views on Salvation in a Pluralistic World* (Grand Rapids, MI: Zondervan, 1995), 12, 95–123. See also: Robert Brow, "Evangelical Megashift,"

Christianity Today, 19 February 1990, 12–14; John G. Stackhouse, Jr., "Evangelicals Reconsider World Religions: Betraying or Affirming the Tradition?" *Christian Century* 110 (8–15 September 1993), 858–65.

Chapter 3

1. John F. Walvoord, *Matthew—Thy Kingdom Come* (Chicago: Moody Press, 1974), 29.

2. Merrill C. Tenney, ed., *Pictorial Encyclopedia of the Bible*, vol. 3 (Grand Rapids, MI: Zondervan, 1976), 644.

3. While it might be argued that Herod's desire to hear the teachings of both John the Baptist and Jesus (Luke 23:8) was laudable, it is clear that Herod's curiosity was merely the reflection of an idle desire to be amused (Luke 23:8–11).

4. George Washington, "To the Hebrew Congregation of the City of Savannah," *Writings*, vol. 31 (May 1790), 42.

5. John Eidsmoe, *Christianity and the Constitution* (Grand Rapids, MI: Baker, 1987), 265, 270.

Chapter 4

1. Francis Schaeffer, *The God Who Is There* (Chicago: Intervarsity Press, 1968), 170.

2. Francis Schaeffer, *The Church at the End of the Twentieth Century* (Downers Grove, IL: Intervarsity Press, 1970), 37.

3. Francis Schaeffer, *The Great Evangelical Disaster* (Westchester, IL: Crossway Books, 1984), 87.

Chapter 5

1. Tony Evans, *The Kingdom Agenda* (Nashville: Word/Thomas Nelson, 1999), 383.

2. Cal Thomas and Ed Dobson, *Blinded by Might* (Grand Rapids, MI: Zondervan, 1999), 118.

3. Norman L. Geisler and Frank S. Turek III, *Legislating Morality* (Minneapolis: Bethany House, 1998), 43.

4. Lewis Sperry Chafer, *Systematic Theology*, vol. IV (Dallas: Dallas Seminary Press, 1948), 45.

Chapter 6

1. Quoted in H. Wayne House and Thomas Ice, *Dominion Theology: Blessing or Curse?—An Analysis of Christian Reconstructionism* (Portland, OR: Multnomah Press, 1988), 419.

2. Garry Wills, *Under God: Religion and American Politics* (New York: Simon and Schuster, 1990), 174.

3. H. Wayne House and Thomas Ice, *Dominion Theology,* 89.

4. Gary DeMar, "Turning the World Upside Down," *Biblical Worldview,* July 1999, 5.

5. *Church of the Holy Trinity v. United States,* 143 U.S. 457, 36 L.Ed. 226 (1892).

Chapter 7

1. Ravi Zacharias, *Deliver Us from Evil: Restoring the Soul in a Disintegrating Culture* (Dallas: Word, 1996), 88.

2. Arthur Lipkin, *Understanding Homosexuality, Changing Schools: A Text for Teachers, Counselors, and Administrators* (Boulder, CO: Westview Press, 1999), xiv–xv.

3. Ibid., 313.

4. Ibid., 317.

Chapter 8

1. Rob Boston, "Family Feud," *Church & State,* May 1998, 14.

2. William Walker, Richard Norris, David Lotz, and Robert Handy, *A History of the Christian Church* (New York: Scribner, 1985), 205.

3. Augustine, *City of God,* book XIX, chapter 26.

4. Ibid.

5. Ibid., book VI, chapter 24.

6. Cal Thomas, "No King but Caesar," *Christianity Today,* May 1999 (advance draft).

7. Charles Van Doren, *A History of Knowledge* (New York: Ballantine Books, 1991), 165.

8. Roland H. Bainton, *The Reformation of the Sixteenth Century* (Boston: Beacon Press, 1952), 242.

9. Ibid.

10. John Calvin (1536), *Institutes of the Christian Religion,* vol. 39 of *Harvard Classics,* Charles W. Eliot, ed. (New York: P. F. Collier & Son, 1910), 31.

11. Bainton, *The Reformation of the Sixteenth Century,* 242.

12. Martin Luther (1520), "Address to the Nobility," *Harvard Classics,* vol. 36, Charles W. Eliot, ed. (New York: P. F. Collier & Son, 1910), 340–350.

Chapter 9

1. Samuel Rutherford, *Lex Rex, or The Law and the Prince: A Dispute for the Just Prerogative of King and People* (Harrisonburg, VA: Sprinkle, 1982 reprint), 189.

2. Thomas Fleming, *Liberty! The American Revolution* (New York: Viking

Press, 1997), 95.

3. Bernard Bailyn, *The Ideological Origins of the American Revolution* (Cambridge, MA: Harvard Press, 1992), 26.

4. Paul Johnson, *A History of the American People* (New York: Harper, 1997), 116.

5. Ibid., 117.

6. Franklin P. Cole, ed., *They Preached Liberty* (Indianapolis: Liberty Press, 1989), preface.

7. Ibid.

8. Ibid., 111.

9. Richard Brookhiser, *Founding Father: Rediscovering George Washington* (New York: The Free Press, 1996), 148.

10. Alexis de Tocqueville, *Democracy in America*, vol. 1, Phillips Bradley, ed. (New York: Vintage Books, 1945), 316–317.

Chapter 10

1. Roger Steer, *Church on Fire: The Story of Anglican Evangelicals* (London: Hodder & Stoughton Ltd., 1998), 225.

2. Edward J. Larson, *Summer of the Gods: The Scopes Trial and America's Continuing Debate over Science and Religion* (New York: Basic Books, 1997), 47.

3. Ibid.

4. Ibid., 146.

5. Ibid., 240.

6. Jerry Falwell, "I'd Do It All Again," *Christianity Today*, 6 September 1999, 51.

Chapter 11

1. *Blinded by Might*, 26.

2. Ibid., 143.

3. Ibid.

4. Ibid., 159.

5. Senator Rick Santorum, "The Necessity of Truth," speech delivered at the Heritage Foundation, Washington, D.C., 29 July 1999.

6. Maggie Gallagher, "Shifting Tide of Abortion Attitudes," *Washington Times*, 24 October 1994, B4.

7. Clarke D. Forsythe, "First Steps: A New Strategy for Pro-Lifers," *National Review*, 20 December 1999, 44.

8. *Planned Parenthood of Southeastern Pennsylvania v. Casey*, 505 U.S. 833 (1992).

9. Elie Pieprz, "Toward Tradition Issues Alert," 12 August 1999, citing the National Right to Life Committee.

10. Ibid., citing Americans United for Life.

11. Andrew Sullivan, "What's So Bad About Hate," *New York Times Magazine*, 26 September 1999, 112.

Chapter 13

1. Leo Pfeffer, *This Honorable Court* (Boston: Beacon Press, 1965) 326, quoting John P. Frank, a biographer of Hugo Black.

2. *Everson v. Board of Education*, 330 U.S. 1 (1947).

3. *1 Annals of Congress*, 434 (8 June 1789).

4. *Abington School District v. Schempp*, 374 U.S. 203 (1963).

5. *Engel v. Vitale*, 370 U.S. 421 (1962).

6. Edward Lazarus, *Closed Chambers: The Rise, Fall, and Future of the Modern Supreme Court* (New York: Penguin Books Ltd., 1999), 332–333.

7. Jonathan Maxcy, "An Oration, Providence, 1799," *American Political Writing During the Foundation Era, 1760–1805*, vol. 2, Charles S. Hyneman and Donald S. Lutz, eds. (Indianapolis: Liberty Press, 1993), 1052.

8. *Committee of Public Education v. Nyquist*, 413 U.S. 756, 820 (1973), White, J., dissenting.

9. *McCollum v. Board of Education*, 333 U.S. 203, 237–38 (1948).

Chapter 14

1. Jill Lawrence, "McCain Backs Off Right-wing Criticism," *USA Today*, 2 March 2000, 1A, 7A.

2. Ibid., 7A.

3. James M. McPherson, *The Abolitionist Legacy: From Reconstruction to the NAACP* (Princeton, NJ: Princeton University Press, 1975), 4–5, 7.

4. Ibid., 10. The smallest representation among the evangelicals belonged to the Quakers. Their beliefs (including reliance on the "inner light") and worship styles (exclusively silent worship) place them outside the category of traditional evangelicals. Nevertheless, they played an important part in voicing moral and spiritual objections to slavery. Furthermore, it is interesting that the more traditional evangelicals apparently had little problem coalescing with the Quakers on this social issue, despite their theological differences.

5. Ibid.

6. Carl N. Degler, *The Other South: Southern Dissenters in the Nineteenth Century* (New York: Harper & Row, 1974), 18.

7. Ibid., 21.

8. Ibid., 28.

9. Ibid., 34.

10. William F. Weld, "Who Is a Republican?" *New York Times,* 14 January 1998, A17.

11. From an address at Cooper Institute, New York, 27 February 1860.

Chapter 15

1. Colin Brown, ed., *Dictionary of New Testament Theology,* vol. 3 (Grand Rapids, MI: Zondervan, 1978), 1165.

Chapter 16

1. "Buchanan on China Vote: 'Ashamed to be a Republican,' " 27 July 1999 press release, Buchanan 2000.

2. John Adams, "Thoughts on Government, Boston, 1776," *American Political Writing During the Foundation Era, 1760–1805,* vol. 1, Charles S. Hyneman and Donald S. Lutz, eds. (Indianapolis: Liberty Press, 1993), 408.

3. Ted Halstead, "A Politics for Generation X," *Atlantic Monthly,* August 1999, 34.

Chapter 17

1. Dan Baltz, "Gore, Bradley and the Soft-Money Shootout," *Washington Post,* 25 July 1999, A06.

2. James W. Marchand, "All Things Work to the Good," *Christian History,* no. 63 (1999), 41.

3. As an example, see predominant photo of Bill Clinton in *U.S. News & World Report,* 13 December 1993, 40 ("Searching for Solace: Bible-toting Bill and Hillary Clinton emerge from Foundry United Methodist Church in Washington, one of three churches they attend regularly").

4. Frank J. Murray, "Clinton Takes 'Ministry' on Crime to Pulpit," *Washington Times,* 15 August 1994, A1.

5. Charles Ryrie, *The Ryrie Study Bible* (Chicago: Moody Press, 1975), 1455.

6. Baron De Montesquieu, transl. Thomas Nugent, *The Spirit of the Laws* (London: Hafner Press/ Collier Macmillan, 1949), xv.

7. Ibid., Vol. II, Book XXIII, 32.

8. Ibid., 21.

9. Richard V. Pierard and Robert D. Linder, *Civil Religion and the Presidency* (Grand Rapids, MI: Zondervan, 1988), 229.

About the Authors

Janet Parshall is host of *Janet Parshall's America,* a nationally syndicated talk show broadcast from Washington, D.C. She is also the chief spokesperson for the Family Research Council. Janet can be seen regularly on the major network news programs. She is a much sought-after speaker who has gained a reputation as one of the most articulate and passionate pro-family advocates in America today. Janet hosts a national radio program, *Renewing the Heart,* for Focus on the Family.

Craig Parshall is a trial lawyer in Virginia who argues cases around the nation involving religious and civil liberties and pro-family issues. He has testified before Congress on issues of constitutional rights and is a frequent debater and writer on matters of faith, freedom, and family.

The Parshalls have been married for twenty-nine years and have four children.